Moments of Crisis in
Jewish – Christian Relations

This volume is presented through the generosity of the Linda Myers Chazen Fund

peace   שלום   שלום

Moments of Crisis in
Jewish – Christian Relations

MARC SAPERSTEIN

SCM PRESS
London

TRINITY PRESS INTERNATIONAL
Philadelphia

First published 1989

SCM Press   Trinity Press International
26–30 Tottenham Road   3725 Chestnut Street
London N1 4BZ   Philadelphia, Pa. 19104

Library of Congress Cataloging-in-Publication Data

Saperstein Marc.
    Moments of crisis in Jewish–Christian relations/Marc Saperstein.
      p. cm.
    ISBN 0–334–01025–X
      1. Judaism–Relations–Christianity. 2. Christianity and other
religions–Judaism. 3. Christianity and antisemitism–History.
    I. Title.
    BM535.S23   1989
    261.2'6'09–dc20   89–37602

British Library Cataloguing in Publication Data

Saperstein, Marc
    Moments of crisis in Jewish–Christian relations.
    1. Christian church. Relations with judaism. 2.
    Judaism. Relations with Christian church
    I.   Title
    261.2'6

ISBN 0–334–01025–X

Photoset by The Spartan Press Ltd, Lymington, Hants
and printed in Great Britain by
Billing & Sons Ltd, Worcester

For my brother, David

Contents

Preface

This book is the result of an invitation by the Chautauqua Institution of Chautauqua, New York, to present five lectures during the summer of 1988 on the history of Jewish–Christian relations. The enthusiastic response to these talks, despite their rather sombre content, encouraged me to seek a publisher for them. I decided to preserve the original form of the lectures, resisting the temptation to expand upon certain issues or to explore their complexity in greater depth, as that would have made this a very different kind of book. Needless to say, it is a work of summary and synthesis rather than innovation, intended for an audience not of scholars but of concerned, thoughtful Christians and Jews who are interested in those aspects of their respective histories and traditions that bear upon the neighbors with whom they have shared a scripture, and much else.

I have supplemented the text of the lectures with notes that substantiate the points made, identify relevant bibliography, and raise associated pertinent issues for further discussion. In most cases, I have limited the bibliographical references to material available in English and accessible in many libraries. It is my hope that the reader will find these notes to be a useful and suggestive complement to the basic text.

I first began to confront systematically the material contained in the following chapters during the course of my graduate work in Jewish history and thought at the Hebrew University and at Harvard. My training was primarily in the medieval period, and I had the good fortune to work with some of the leading authorities in the field, including Professors Haim Hillel Ben-Sasson, Jacob Katz, Isador Twersky, and Yosef Yerushalmi. Their insights and their approach to the texts that are the raw material of historical knowledge have been internalized to the point where I cannot always define my indebtedness.

From my initial orientation in the Middle Ages, I began to move both earlier and later in the history of Jewish–Christian relations. Among the most stimulating and rewarding responsibilities in my position on the faculty of the Harvard Divinity School, where I taught Jewish Studies from 1979–1986, was to offer a seminar together with Professor Krister Stendahl entitled "Jews and Christians: the Perception of the Other." I learned from Krister Stendahl's deep erudition pertaining to the New Testament, his vast experience in all aspects of contemporary Jewish–Christian relations, his uncanny ability to understand and articulate the perspective of the Other, and his irrepressible penchant to cut through all forms of sanctimonious cant. Confronting with students the anti-Jewish diatribes of Martin Luther in the presence of this distinguished Lutheran scholar and theologian provided me with a model of the honest soul-searching necessary for authentic dialogue.

After Krister Stendahl left Harvard to become Bishop of Stockholm, I taught the same course together with Professor John Townsend of the Episcopal Divinity School; my education in matters relating to the New Testament and Christian origins continued with him. Nevertheless, I have bypassed the difficult questions relating to the teachings and career of Jesus of Nazareth in my presentation. As important as these questions are for contemporary Jewish–Christian relations, they belong to a discipline in which I can claim no expertise, and they pertain to a period in which one cannot as yet speak about two distinct religions. I have begun my account with the parting of ways, leaving the "historical Jesus" and the Jewish movement that coalesced around him during his lifetime to others who can address such subjects more authoritatively.

Upon coming to Washington University in 1986 as the Gloria M. Goldstein Professor of Jewish History and Thought, I began to investigate more systematically the vast array of materials pertaining to the Holocaust. Because of my prior training, I view the Holocaust against the broad canvas of Jewish historical experience, interested particularly in the question of continuities and discontinuities with the past. My presentation in the fourth chapter focuses on one aspect of this vast topic – not the development and implementation of the Nazi program of genocide, nor the spectrum of Jewish responses to the harrowing circumstances that confronted European Jewry, but the reactions of Christians who were self-consciously speaking and acting out of their tradition to the attempted destruction of the Jewish people.

Throughout my presentation, I have aspired toward the historian's goal of detachment. Drawing from the best available scholarly research, I have attempted not to advocate, judge, or condemn, but rather to reconstruct the range of options facing individuals in their own historical contexts, to explain insofar as possible the reasons for the choices that were made, and to assess the implications of such decisions for subsequent developments. I recognize, however, that the ideal of objectivity in historical writing is illusionary, for fundamental decisions about the selection and organization of one's material necessarily entail value judgments. The historian's position is particularly precarious in moving, as I have done in my final chapter, from the past to the present. It is therefore appropriate to articulate my own commitments and the preconceptions that may inform the material to follow.

I am a rabbi in the liberal, Reform branch of Judaism, and an academic trained in the critical analysis of historical sources. I am committed to the survival and flourishing of the Jewish people both in the Diaspora and its ancestral homeland, though I do not consider myself to be a spokesman for any political position or to use historical arguments for any ideological goal. I reject the notion, found occasionally in traditional Jewish literature, that conflict and enmity are the natural paradigm for the relationship between Jews and Gentiles. I believe that a full and balanced confrontation with the record of the past in all its horrors is a necessary precondition for honest and open relations in the present, yet I also believe that those living today bear no responsibility for the misdeeds of their ancestors, and that guilt cannot serve as a solid foundation for any healthy relationship.

I am deeply concerned about the resurgence of fundamentalist, fanatical, extremist views not only within Islam and Christianity but also within contemporary Judaism, often justified by appeals to Jewish texts and claims to be the only "authentic" Judaism. These claims seem to me to be ethically barren, politically dangerous, and intellectually dishonest. I am impressed by the diversity of sources in both the Jewish and the Christian traditions, each containing elements of universalistic openness toward the Other, and also of suspicion and hostility which sees all good within one's own camp, and outside that camp at best nothing of value and at worst the forces of the demonic. Neither one of these strands has a clear *prima facie* claim for authenticity; which one is emphasized and expressed at any historical juncture is, for better or for worse, the result of the decisions of human beings, who may believe that they are acting in accordance with God's will, but who may very well be mistaken. My understanding of the historical record described below is that it demonstrates the capacity of decent, sincere, religious people for cruelty, stupidity, and callous indifference to the suffering others, but also for sacrificial devotion to the most ennobling of values.

I want to express my gratitude to the Chautauqua Institution for providing the occasion and the context in which the following material reached its present form; to my father, Rabbi Harold Saperstein, my Washington University colleague Peter Riesenberg, and members of the St Louis Rabbinical Association, for their careful reading and astute criticisms of all or parts of my manuscript; and to the many students at Harvard and Washington University who have pondered this material with me and pressed me to clarify, rethink, and probe more deeply.

The Institute for Advanced Studies   Marc Saperstein
Jerusalem 1989

I

Jews and Christians in Antiquity:
A Reversal of Power

Frequently we assume that history had to be the way it was, as if it all followed a pre-ordained course. Particularly in the field of religion, the decisions that were made and the events that occurred seem in retrospect to be necessary and self-evident. Often they were not. Before the die is cast, there are often several plausible and attractive alternatives, buttressed by compelling arguments and powerful supporters. Only by understanding these alternatives can we appreciate the significance of the choice actually made. In the early history of Christianity, at least four fundamental questions challenged leaders of the church, and each of these questions would have enormous implications for the course of Christian–Jewish relations. I will touch briefly upon the first three, then linger on the fourth.

A first major question concerns identity, definition, and the line of demarcation between the two groups. Near the very beginning of what scholars call the "Jesus Movement," before there was any church, the question arose in the form "Must a Christian observe the Mosaic commandments?" or, to put it differently, "Do you have to be a Jew to be a Christian?" Today the question seems trivial, almost absurd. To those Jews who continued to believe in their messiah even after the scandal of the cross (cf. I Cor. 1:23), the answer was by no means obvious. They knew, of course, that Jesus had lived his entire life as a Jew. They also knew that his career was devoted entirely to

Jews, that he seems to have had little if any interest in preaching to Gentiles. The idea that one could become a follower of Jesus, a believer in Jesus, without first becoming a Jew seemed to some of the disciples a ludicrous perversion of the master's teaching.[1]

If their view had prevailed, the history of the West would have taken a radically different course, and our subject would not exist. Christianity might never have become a separate religion but rather remained within the context of Judaism, possibly as a distinct Jewish sect, possibly reabsorbed with some of its teachings woven into the broad fabric of Jewish doctrine. But following the fateful "Council of Jerusalem" (Acts 15), adherents of the alternative controlled the evangelistic agenda. Having failed to make substantial inroads within the Jewish community, Jewish followers of Jesus began to seek Gentile adherents to their faith without requiring conversion to Judaism, and they found increasing success in their mission. Christianity thus became largely a religion of Gentiles. Jews who came to it were the exception, not the rule; the conversion of the Jews *en masse* remained, at least in most periods of history, a Christian aspiration, not a reality.

The problem of identity was not, however, fully resolved by the decision to welcome Gentiles directly into the new faith. As we see in Paul's Epistle to the Galatians, a new aspect of this problem arose: "*May* a Christian observe the practices of the Jews?" If Gentiles could become Christians, then clearly observance of the law was not essential for salvation. But what about those Gentile Christians who were attracted to the ancient rituals observed by their messiah; what about those Jewish Christians who wanted to continue their traditional practices in their new faith? Was it *permissible* for them to observe the Sabbath on the seventh day, keep the dietary laws, practice circumcision? Could those who acknowledged Jesus but observed the law of Moses hope for salvation?

In the second century, this was still an open question. Justin Martyr states that he would accept those who continue to observe the commandments into Christian fellowship, providing they do not seek to convince Gentile Christians to follow the Mosaic law, but he admits that others reject the openness of his view.[2] By the fourth century, however, church authorities had

2

excluded this option. Observing the Mosaic commandments, or "Judaizing," was determined to be a heresy, not only for Gentile Christians but even for Jewish converts.[3] Many would suffer the consequences of that ruling.

A second fundamental question pertained to scripture. Christians had to decide: "Is the Hebrew Bible part of our sacred text?" This question could not have arisen at the beginnings of the church, for the Hebrew Bible was then the only scripture Christians recognized. Not until a selection of Gospels and Epistles and other literary texts about the life and significance of Jesus coalesced into a new scripture did the problem of the relationship with the traditional, classical scripture engender controversy.

Here, too, the outcome was by no means self-evident. A position that many found plausible and some compelling was formulated by Marcion, one of the most profoundly provocative Christian thinkers of antiquity. He held that the Old Testament had been totally replaced by the New, that the God of the Old Testament was not the Christian God but an evil being whose commandments were intended to enslave.[4] Anyone who has experienced surprise encounters with robust sexuality, or primitive violence, or cynical political intrigue in the pages of Hebrew scripture will understand why Marcion's purism had a powerful appeal. It took vigorous efforts by church leaders to repudiate it.

That the legacy of Marcion was not totally suppressed can be seen in various Christian tendencies to subordinate or denigrate the Old Testament. It erupted in full force once again in the 1930s, when a group of German Christians under the Nazi regime denounced the Old Testament as a book of "Jewish lying and deceit."[5] But the position of the church was clear: Marcion was declared a heretic, and the Hebrew Bible was salvaged as Christian scripture. The normative Christian doctrine asserting continuity between the two Testaments recognized that the Jews of antiquity were indeed God's chosen people. Jews were not thrilled by the Christian appropriation of their Bible,[6] but the Gnostic demonization of the Old Testament might well have made matters considerably worse.[7]

A third fundamental question concerned sacred space: "Is the land of Israel our 'Holy Land'?" Unlike the previous questions, here there was no official solution and ambivalence lingered.

During the first three Christian centuries the tendency was to minimize the significance of the land of Israel and Jerusalem. The very category of "holy space" was somewhat suspect. Jewish attachment to sacred geography was viewed with some condescension, as typical of the "carnal" worldview that Christianity had transcended. This changed in the fourth century, when Christian emperors first ruled over the Holy Land. Pilgrimage to the sacred site emerged as a recognized religious value.[8]

That opened up a new area of competition between Christians and Jews, who viewed Christian sovereignty over Palestine as no improvement over that of the pagan Romans. The tradition of spiritualization was so firmly rooted in the beginnings of Christianity that the territorial dimension could never become as pronounced in Christian piety as it was in Judaism.[9] Nevertheless, the idea of a "Holy Land," launched in the fourth century, was never fully abandoned. Tensions over this issue erupted again in the High Middle Ages with the proclamation of the Crusades, and in the twentieth century against the background of modern Zionism.

The fourth issue was the most crucial for the Jews. This was the question of toleration: "Should Jews be permitted to live as Jews under Christian rule? If so, what should be the ground rules of such tolerance?" The very formulation of this question presupposes a dramatic reversal in the power relations between the two communities. It is frequently forgotten that in the period of Christian origins, the Jews were a major power – not, to be sure, a superpower in the category of Rome or Parthian Persia, but a power to be reckoned with nonetheless. Numbering some seven million in the middle of the first century, Jews constituted ten per cent of the population of the entire Roman Empire; in the eastern Mediterranean this was substantially higher.[10] When Judea revolted against Rome in the years 66 and 132, elite Roman legions had to be transferred from Europe to suppress the Jewish armies. No other nation within the Empire posed such a thorny military problem for Rome.

These revolts were disastrous for the Jews. The first led to the fall of Jerusalem and the destruction of the Temple, the second to the virtual annihilation of the Jewish population in Judea. Hardly a settlement was allowed to remain. Although Galilee did not suffer nearly as much, the Jewish population of the land of Israel was reduced by more than half a million during the four years of the second revolt, and so many Jews were sold into slavery that the price of slaves plummeted throughout the Empire. On the site of the Temple the Romans built a pagan shrine; Jerusalem, renamed Aelia Capitolina in honor of the emperor Hadrian and the god Jupiter, became officially *Judenrein*.[11]

These devastating blows broke the backbone of Jewish military power, yet they did not destroy the Jewish people. The Romans deemed Judaism to be a "legal religion," and from the year 212 Jews were formally recognized as citizens of the Roman Empire. Flourishing Jewish communities were scattered throughout the Mediterranean basin – in North Africa, Asia Minor, Greece, and Rome itself, not to mention Babylonia. By contrast, the faith which began to be called Christianity was not recognized as legal by Rome.[12] Its adherents remained, at least through the second century, a small, persecuted sect. On levels perhaps too deep to be fully articulated, they must have looked upon Jews with a certain amount of envy.

Without remembering this power relationship, the original thrust of some polemical literature may be misunderstood. Melito, bishop of Sardis in the second century, bequeathed to posterity a Homily on the Pascha (the coincidence of Passover and Good Friday) in which the charge of deicide, the murder of God, is for the first time recorded. Listen to his attack upon the Jewish people:

> Lawless Israel, why have you done this new wrong and brought new suffering upon the Lord, your Master, your Maker, upon him who honored you, who called you Israel? . . . Him whom the nations worshipped and whom the uncircumcised admired and the Gentiles glorified, for whom even Pilate washed his hand, him have you slain in the great feast. Therefore bitter to you shall be the feast of unleavened bread . . . You have slain your Lord in the midst of Jerusalem. Hear all you families of man, and see [the strange murder] that has been committed . . . He who hung the earth in its place is hanged, he who fixed the heavens is

fixed upon the cross . . . the Master has been insulted, God has been murdered, the King of Israel has been slain by an Israelite hand.[13]

The original context in which these words were spoken was illuminated in 1962 by excavations at Sardis, about sixty miles from the western coast of Asia Minor. To everyone's amazement, the archaeologists unearthed a magnificent synagogue, 130 yards long, adorned with elegant marble and impressive mosaics, on the main street of the city, something like Saint Patrick's Cathedral in New York. The Christian church was much smaller and in a less desirable location.[14] Melito was not, then, an oppressor attacking those who were down and out; he was trying to convince his people that the feast of Passover had been superseded and the Jews rejected by God despite appearances to the contrary.

Even in the latter half of the fourth century, when the power relationship between the two groups had radically shifted, the image of Jews as harried adherents of a humiliated and spurned faith bears little relation to reality. Perhaps the churchman who did more than any other individual in antiquity to stock the arsenal of anti-Jewish invective was the great preacher of Antioch, St John Chrysostom, "the man with the golden mouth," the most eloquent among the fathers of the Eastern church. Here is Chrysostom addressing his congregation about the Jews:

> If [the Jews] are ignorant of the Father, if they crucified the Son, and spurned the aid of the Spirit, cannot one declare with confidence that the synagogue is a dwelling place of demons? God is not worshipped there. Far from it! Rather, the synagogue is a temple of idolatry . . . A synagogue is less honorable than any inn. For it is not simply a gathering place for thieves and hucksters, but also of demons. Indeed, not only the synagogue, but the soul of Jews are also the dwelling places of demons.[15]

Chrysostom's sermons often reveal a preacher swept away by the power of his own rhetoric. But the context is important. The purpose of these anti-Jewish sermons is to criticize members of his church who are attending the local synagogue during the holidays of Passover and Yom Kippur. The fever pitch of this polemic against the synagogue therefore testifies to the appeal of the synagogue, with its rituals rooted in the calendar of Hebrew Scripture, for Christians in late fourth-century Antioch. Repugnant as they sound, these are not the words of a man calling his listeners to acts of violence and destruction against the Jews, but rather the words of a leader troubled that his people were attracted by the aura of a religion more ancient and in some ways more venerable than his own. In the popular mind, at least, the fundamental question of identity – of Christians observing Jewish practices – had not yet been fully resolved.

By this time, however, the forces were in place that would eventually consign the Jews to a position of vulnerability and make such words as those of Melito and Chrysostom considerably more dangerous than they were when first uttered. The decisive turning point, one of the most important events in the history of the West, was the unexpected (and never fully explained) conversion to Christianity of the Emperor Constantine in the year 312, leading to the eventual emergence of Christianity as the official religion of the Empire. For better or for worse, Christianity became wedded to politics, and we need to assess the effect of this marriage upon the relations between Christians and Jews.

The unanticipated accession to the pinnacles of world power had considerable impact upon Christian thought. Now that the meek had inherited the earth, doctrines of martyrdom and suffering servanthood were supplanted by an ideology of triumphalism, which identified victory and success upon the stage of history as irrefutable evidence of divine approval. The power of imperial Rome, earlier viewed at best as a bulwark of stability but more frequently as the impetus for persecution, now became the sign of God's favor. And the status of the Jewish people moved beyond the realm of apologetical literature into the realm of legislation, a matter which Christians were able not merely to argue about but to control.

Yet the dramatic shift in the fortunes of Christianity did not produce a precipitous decline in the fortunes of Jews. Jewish status was governed by Roman law, which remained intact under the Christian Emperors. The conservative nature of this great legal system mitigated against the total and sudden disenfranchisement of a substantial minority. The position of the Jews was therefore modified piecemeal, bit by bit; their status remained the same, but specific legislation imposed particular restrictions. The first of these, promulgated by Constantine himself (probably in 329), forbade Jews to accept converts from Christianity or to prevent their own people from becoming Christians.[16] The earlier enthusiasm of Jews for proselytization rapidly diminished once it was against the law.

Yet though most of the rights enjoyed by Jews as Roman citizens were not immediately abolished, the implications of the new relationship were clear. For the first time, Christians had the power to eliminate Judaism completely from much of the Western world. Nor was this impossible to conceive. Some churchmen argued that all who diverged from the true doctrine should be vigorously suppressed. In order to appreciate the significance of continued Jewish life in a Christian *imperium*, it is therefore necessary to compare the fate of the Jews with that of two other groups: pagans and heretics.

Paganism – not just the old-fashioned myths of the ancient pantheon but the sophisticated philosophical paganism of Plotinus and Porphyry and the mystery cults – continued to represent a serious intellectual challenge to fourth-century Christians. Constantine's own policy has been characterized as a "carefully moderated antipathy," but his successors clamped down hard, prohibiting sacrifices in 341 and (after the resurgence during the reign of the pagan emperor Julian) again in 381, and unleashing waves of persecution by Christian fanatics. Emperors who imposed particular restrictions on Jewish privileges were far more ruthless in their attempts to suppress pagan worship. Paganism was powerful and resilient, and its great centers in Italy, Greece, and Egypt were not easily destroyed, but by the sixth century, its strength had been broken by the onslaught of Justinian's repressive measures.[17]

Even greater vindictiveness was shown toward those whom the church branded as "heretics." Here too we are speaking about policy not toward licentious atheists, but toward deeply religious men and women who happened to differ on a particular theological formulation from those whose doctrine carried the day. Constantine attempted to legislate an end to all heretical sects, announcing that their places of meeting would be confiscated. A general anti-heretical law was promulgated by the emperor Gratian in 379, and Theodosius intensified the repression in what has been termed a "legislative juggernaut." Uniformity was not imposed overnight, but as one scholar has put it, "During the fourth century, the wheel had turned the full circle. From being the persecuted, the Christians were now the persecutors." Christians who deviated theologically knew that they would feel the scourge of imperial power. Within a century of Constantine's conversion, most of the great "heresies" of antiquity had been drastically diminished.[18]

It was certainly not beyond the imagination that similar policies could have been applied to the Jews. St Ambrose, Bishop of Milan, apparently favored such a course, and he was not alone.[19] After all, why should Jews, who rejected everything sacred to Christianity, be tolerated, while Christians who deviated on one theological detail were not? A theory was needed that would define the status of Jews within a Christian realm, providing an unambiguous answer to the question, "Should Jews be permitted to live as Jews in our midst?" Such a theory was articulated by St Augustine of Hippo. Elsewhere in his work, Augustine provided intellectual justification and scriptural support for the state's persecution of Christian heretics.[20] His treatment of the Jews was quite different, and it had such enormous influence for almost 1400 years that it is worth lingering to summarize its major features.[21]

Augustine argued not only that Jews should be permitted to live in a Christian realm, but also that their continued existence as a people was desired by God and served a positive function in Christian life. How so? Jews were valuable first as the "guardians of scripture." In the ongoing debate between Christians and pagans, Christians had to counter the charge that their faith was an innovation lacking roots in the past. They therefore insisted that it was rooted in prophecies contained in an ancient text – the Hebrew Bible – which were fulfilled in the life of Jesus. But what if it was maintained that the Christians fabricated and interpolated these passages to make it seem as if ancient prophecies were being fulfilled? The Jews serve as witness to the authenticity of the texts that Christians cite. These Jews certainly have no interest in strengthening the Christian case, yet their own copies of the Bible reveal that the prophecies providing a foundation for the Christian claim are genuine.

Second, Augustine affirmed that Jews are living proof of the truth of Christian faith. Centuries ago, they had committed the unpardonable sin – defying God by rejecting his messiah. They were therefore punished and have borne the consequences ever since: defeat, exile, subjugation. Others, including Christians, who might consider rejecting the Christ can be warned with an object-lesson: look at the Jews; do you want a similar fate? If Jews were to disappear from Christian society, this powerful lesson might be reduced to an easily overlooked antiquarian footnote. So long as they are preserved they serve as a continuously present reminder of the wages of sin. In this sense, Augustine applied the biblical verse "Slay them [i.e., the Jews] not, lest my people [i.e., the Christians] forget; Make them wander to and fro' (Ps. 59.12).

To buttress this point, Augustine resorted to typology, a mode of biblical interpretation which explains characters in the Bible as foreshadowing later events. Cain and Abel were brothers. Both brought offerings to God, but the offering of Cain was rejected. He killed his brother. God's punishment was to make him a "fugitive and wanderer [in the Vulgate: groaning and trembling] upon the earth." But God warned that Cain must not be killed by any human being, and set a mark upon him so that all would recognize that he was, though cursed, under God's protection.[22]

So it was with the Jews. Their offerings had ceased to be acceptable to God. They killed their brother, Jesus. They were punished by being sent into exile, made into fugitives and wanderers, groaning and trembling. But they were also given a mark of identification – the sign of circumcision – so that all would know that God did not want this people to be killed.

St Augustine's theory of the meaning of Jewish existence would become the foundation of official church doctrine, cited by popes and other churchmen throughout the Middle Ages. Note that it has two components. It insists upon physical safety for the Jews: they are not to be put to death. But it also insists that in order to fulfil their function, Jews must live under conditions that would demonstrate their reprobate character and attest to their status of being accursed. For Jews to enjoy a higher standard of living than Christians, or for Jews to hold a position of authority over Christians, would violate the ground rules of toleration.

In later centuries, various popes emphasized one or the other of these provisions as the situation demanded. To those who rose up violently against Jews, they reiterated the verse from Psalms: "Slay them not." To kings or nobles who allowed Jews to prosper economically or become too influential, they frequently demanded that the Jews be kept in their proper place.[23] Which of these two aspects of the official doctrine was more important in determining the welfare of the Jews? It may be argued that on the whole, the commitment to physical safety was more significant than the call for economic and social deprivation, which was often ignored. There is a heavy tinge of irony in the statement by Moses Mendelssohn: "Blessed be the ashes of that humane theologian [Augustine] who was the first to declare that God was preserving us as a visible proof of the Nazarene religion. But for this lovely brainwave, we would have been exterminated long ago."[24] Yet there is also more than a grain of truth.

Up to this point, our discussion has focused upon Christian doctrines concerning the Jews. What about the other side of the ledger? It is somewhat surprising to note how little explicit reference to Christianity is contained in the substantial literature of the first five centuries collected in the two Talmuds and various works of Midrash. It may be, as has been recently argued, that the accession of a Christian as emperor and the transformation of Christianity into a faith buttressed by imperial power lies behind fourth-century rabbinic thinking on such fundamental issues as the meaning of history, the nature of messianic redemption, and the identity of the people of Israel.[25]

But these are answers for questions that are nowhere articulated. Christianity is not confronted directly in the rabbinic texts as Judaism is in the writings of Justin Martyr, Eusebius, Chrysostom and Augustine. Esau and Edom, familiar types for Rome in early rabbinic texts, were simply transferred to Christianity as if no significant break had occurred. Constantine is not mentioned in the rabbinic literature; even the thrilling though ultimately abortive attempt to rebuild the Temple under the pagan emperor Julian leaves only the vaguest echo.[26] It was not until the twelfth century that a Jewish historian endeavored to assess the significance of Constantine for Christianity.[27]

What the rabbis and other Jews actually thought about Christianity, and whether their silence resulted from fear of reprisal or a refusal to concede recognition to the newly formidable adversary, we cannot know. The fact is that the classical texts from the formative period of rabbinic Judaism give no explicit evidence that Christianity was perceived as a major problem. These texts contain a few extremely hostile statements about Jesus and Mary, statements attributed to individuals and lacking any official status (though they caused no end of trouble once they became known, through apostates, in the thirteenth century).[28] Only one New Testament verse is quoted in the Talmud, not surprisingly a statement congenial with Judaism: "I have not come to diminish the Law of Moses, nor to add to it" (B.Shab 116a–b, cf. Matt. 5:17–18).

We do find in the rabbinic literature a host of statements about Gentiles, primarily legislation attempting to enforce social and religious segregation.[29] But in this literature, as in the Bible itself, the Gentiles mentioned were pagans engaged in idolatrous worship. Furthermore, the laws were intended for a situation in which Jews were a majority in their own land and could avoid contact with Gentiles without severe economic consequences. When the two underlying premises of this legislation changed, when the Gentiles in question worshipped the same God as did the Jews, and when Jews began to live as a minority on foreign soil, these rules became extremely problematic. In short, Jewish thinkers of antiquity never developed an articulated doctrine of Christianity as Christian thinkers did of Judaism and the Jewish people. In confronting the new medieval reality, the only guidance Jews could find in their classical literature would turn out to be a source of consternation and embarassment.

But before moving on to the Middle Ages, it is worth raising one final question. What would have been the course of Western civilization, and of Christian–Jewish relations, if at that fateful moment Constantine had converted not to Christianity but to Judaism, making Judaism the religion of empire and leaving Christianity a small sect fighting for the right of toleration? Would there have been substantially more brotherhood and less persecution in the subsequent centuries? Or would power have corrupted the victors, no matter who they were? Hypothetical questions are not susceptible to definitive answers, but the study of history and of contemporary events provides a strong basis for arguing that no religious tradition and no religious people is immune to the poison of fanaticism. The evidence suggests that especially within a monotheistic context, the zeal of genuine commitment and faith is all too easily transmuted into bigotry toward those who are different, and that the presence or absence of power may well be the most important factor determining whether such bigotry will lead to persecution. The implications of this thought will have to be assessed as our account of moments of crisis in Jewish – Christian relations after Constantine and Augustine continues.

2

The High Middle Ages:
Violence and a Persecuting Society

We have seen that in the critical period following the establishment of Christianity as the religion of the Empire – a period
in which the fate of the Jewish people for centuries to come was
determined – St Augustine, the most profound and influential
thinker among the fathers of the Latin church, formulated
doctrines which justified both persecution of Christian heretics
and toleration of Jews. The only condition was that the Jews
remain politically and socially subservient to their Christian
neighbors. During the early Middle Ages, this doctrine
emerged from the realms of theology and hermeneutics to enter
the domain of law, incorporated into papal legislation that
would guide the church for centuries. The first major figure in
this process was the greatest of the early medieval popes,
Gregory I.

The principle that Jews were to be tolerated and not
subjected to violent oppression was given concrete form in a
powerfully repercussive decision relating to the thorny problem of forced baptism. It was occasioned by a formal protest
addressed to Pope Gregory in the year 591 by the Jews of
Rome on behalf of their co-religionists in southern France.
According to the Pope's own understatement, these Jews had
been "brought to the font of baptism more by force than by
preaching." Whatever their associations with the papacy as
pre-eminent symbol of a rival faith, politically the Roman
Jews identified the Pope not as the enemy but as an important

ally, and the Lateran Palace as the appropriate address for their complaint.

Gregory responded in a letter to the bishops of Arles and Marseilles,[1] gently admonishing that despite the noble purpose of winning new souls, force must not be sanctioned. He argues that even if the intentions of the zealots are commendable – to save the benighted Jews – the forced baptism, devoid of any scriptural support, is counterproductive. Here is how he puts it: "When any one is brought to the font of baptism not by the sweetness of preaching but by compulsion, he returns to his former superstition, and dies the worse from having been born again" – a sentence rich with assumptions and implications that need to be unpacked.

Judaism is characterized here, as frequently in Gregory's letters, as a "superstition," a term which originally had more to do with the legal status of a cult than with the substance of belief.[2] The central argument is not theological but psychological: those who are not convinced but compelled will feel no loyalty to the new faith, and as soon as an opportunity presents itself they will return to their accustomed ways. But note what else is implied. Even though it is improperly effected and lacks full consent, the baptism is valid, and it is indelible. Those who were baptized have become Christians and must remain so for the rest of their lives.[3] If they return to the practice of Judaism, they can no longer be considered Jews; they must be considered Christians guilty of the heresy of Judaizing. And that is a much more serious matter.

Gregory's letter speaks only of the fate of the soul: God will punish the Christian heretic more severely than the Jew, and the effect of baptism will therefore be the opposite of what was intended, ultimately hurting rather than helping the convert. In the following centuries, the dire institutional consequences would become clear. Heresy remained a matter on which the medieval church found no room for compromise. As Thomas Aquinas put it, heretics "deserve not only to be separated from the church by excommunication, but also to be severed from the world by death."[4] The church dealt with heresy through the Inquisition, an ecclesiastical court that had no jurisdiction over Jews *per se*, but did have jurisdiction over Jews who had been baptized, even under duress. Jews as Jews were entitled to observe all their ancient traditions without being disturbed; but a Jew who had been baptized and observed even a single Jewish practice or professed a single Jewish belief could be prosecuted, and burnt at the stake.

That, however, was all in the future. For some five centuries after Gregory I, Jews settled in Europe and were, on the whole, left alone. The one major exception was in Visigothic Spain during the seventh century, where a radically different policy was essayed, including a royal edict mandating compulsory baptism of all the Jews in the realm – just twenty-two years after Gregory's letter![5] This experience dramatically points to what might have been the fate of all Jews in Europe but was not. For most rulers, it was the road not taken. Charlemagne spread the Gospel by the sword in northern Europe, compelling the pagan Saxons to accept baptism under penalty of death, but he was well-disposed toward the Jews, particularly encouraging Jewish merchant activity. A recent study has concluded that of several hundred European rulers and sixty-seven popes over a period of four centuries in the early Middle Ages, only a dozen appear to have had an anti-Jewish policy.[6]

Many of them, recognizing the value of Jewish communities, followed a policy that was vigorously and consistently pro-Jewish. In their realms, Jews prospered, enjoying a legal status not materially different from that of their Christian neighbors. They owned land, engaged in a wide range of professions and occupations (including agriculture, the military, and public office), and in general lived next to Christians without noticeable popular antipathy. The complaints of various churchmen – for example that the Jewish women of Lyons dress as lavishly as the ladies of the court, or that Christians prefer to hear the sermons of Jewish preachers and neglect their own clergy – seem to have had little effect on the secular rulers. The Jewish communities were small, to be sure, but thriving.[7]

The year 1096 is one of those dates that serve historians as a convenient demarcation for the beginning of a new era. Certainly the armies marching from France and Germany under the banner of the cross to free the Holy Land from the infidel represented a new and stirring ideal in Christendom. But while the word "Crusade" has many positive associations in Christian ears – devotion to and sacrifice for the faith, fighting for the honor of the Savior – its resonance in Jewish consciousness is quite different. In the minds of many, it is the first in a litany of persecutions that serve as a mythic paradigm of Jewish life under Christian rule.

According to contemporary accounts, Pope Urban II's proclamation of a Crusade at the Council of Clermont emphasized the special sanctity of Jerusalem, the desecration or destruction of Christian holy places, and the suffering of pilgrims to the Holy Land, thereby reaffirming the importance of sacred real estate in Christian spirituality. There is no evidence that the speech contained any anti-Jewish component.[8] In the official launching of a world war over the Holy Land, the Jews were more or less forgotten. The Pope's speech, however, did contain expressions of contempt for the Turks, and the anti-Muslim sentiment, fanned by religious, millenarian fervor, was not easy to control.

The Jews of the Rhineland were considerably more accessible, more vulnerable, and more familiar as villains from the Christian scripture than the exotic Muslim enemy, and some Crusaders found it difficult to understand why one infidel should be destroyed and the other left in peace. This is the import of the statement attested in Jewish and Christian sources alike: "We are marching a great distance to seek our sanctuary and to take vengeance on the Muslims. Lo and behold, there live among us Jews whose forefathers slew [Jesus] and crucified him for no cause. Let us revenge ourselves on them first and eliminate them from among the nations, so that the name of Israel no longer be remembered, or else let them be like ourselves and believe in [the Christ]."[9] This last option may have been motivated by the popular belief that the millenarian drama of battle with the armies of the Antichrist, which was beginning with the Crusade, must also include the conversion of the Jews.[10]

Against this threat, the Jews were not defenseless, nor were they without allies. Their safety and security had been guaranteed in 1090 by Henry IV, Emperor of all the Romans, in a charter addressed to "all the bishops, abbots, dukes and counts . . . of our kingdom." As the Crusader armies began their march through the Rhineland, the Emperor, residing in

Italy, issued a stern warning that the Jews of his realm were not to be harmed.[11] Some of the largest Crusader armies, under the leadership of Peter the Hermit and Godfrey of Bouillon, passed through the area without incident. When the situation began to look dangerous, local bishops in Speyer, Worms and Mainz invited Jews into their fortified castles and tried to defend them with their own men at arms. The Jews were also prepared to fight in their own self-defense, and did so; according to the primary Hebrew chronicle, they were led by their rabbi, Kalonymos ben Meshullam.

Then the dam burst. Crusaders under the banner of Count Emicho of Leisingen broke through the ramparts of the bishop's palace in Mainz and overpowered Christian and Jewish defenders alike, sometimes massacring out of control, sometimes giving a choice of baptism or death. The Jews, realizing that this story would have no happy outcome, reacted in different ways: some accepted baptism in order to save their lives, some refused and prepared to be killed as martyrs, some decided to anticipate the Crusaders by taking the lives of their children and killing themselves in mass communal suicide. A similar pattern was repeated in other cities of the Rhineland. The number of deaths is estimated by scholars as approximately 5000, not large by twentieth-century standards, but a devastating blow for the Jews of the region.[12]

Did this represent a fundamental shift in Jewish–Christian relations?[13] No, and yes. The Emperor established his good faith by trying to intercede on behalf of the Jews; later, he permitted those converted under duress to return to Judaism, in violation of established church doctrine.[14] Bishops made a genuine effort to protect the Jews in their domain, in some cases at risk to their own lives. The massacres and the forced conversions were clearly a violation of papal policy. Medieval popes were prepared to launch crusades against Muslims, and later even against Christian heretics, but never against Jews.

When in the Second Crusade the German Jews were again threatened, no less a figure than St Bernard of Clairvaux, perhaps the most universally admired and influential Christian of the twelfth century, traveled to the Rhineland to appeal for their safety. His argument, as it appears in his own writings, was taken straight from Augustine.

> The Jews are not to be persecuted, killed, or even put to flight. Ask anyone who knows the sacred scripture what he finds foretold of the Jews in the Psalms. "Nor for their destruction do I pray," it says (Ps. 59:12). The Jews are for us the living words of scripture, for they remind us always of what our Lord suffered. They are dispersed all over the world so that by expiating their crime they may be everywhere the living witnesses of our redemption. Hence the same Psalm adds, "only let thy power disperse them." . . . If the Jews are utterly wiped out, what will become of our hope for their promised salvation, their eventual conversion?[15]

According to both Jewish and Christian sources, his intervention successfully prevented further bloodshed.

Nevertheless, there are grounds for seeing the anti-Jewish violence of the Crusades as symbolic, if not symptomatic, of a profound change. The massacres revealed that lower levels of Christian society could not be counted upon to behave toward the Jews as official doctrine taught, that popular antipathy could be stirred up by lesser clergy and spill over into violence unsanctioned by king or pope. From the Jewish side, this antipathy was fervently reciprocated; the Hebrew chronicles of the Crusades are filled with expressions of contempt for all that Christians hold sacred. The biblical imprecation "Pour out your wrath upon the nations that do not know you" (Ps. 79:6) was incorporated into the Passover Haggadah at this time. New systems of Jewish thought would emerge in which all contact with Christians was viewed as dangerous and sullying.[16] The cross, the symbol in which the massacres were perpetrated, acquired powerful negative associations for Jews that linger to this day.[17] The trauma of 1096 was not easily dissipated, particularly since it augured heightened tensions ahead.

Some fifty years later, a second symbolic or symptomatic event, with even more sinister repercussions, would occur. The year was 1144. In the English city of Norwich, a child named William was murdered near the time of Easter, apparently stabbed to death. A story was circulated that Jews of Norwich were responsible. Not much credence was given to the story at first, but it was not forgotten, and a few years later it was revived. Five years after his death, the body of William was reburied in the cathedral as martyr and saint and, much to the delight of the local merchants, the burial place became a shrine.

The entire story was recounted by a monk named Thomas of Monmouth in a book called *De vita et passione sancti Willelmi Martyris Norvicensis*, The Life and Passion of the Martyr St William of Norwich, a fascinating mixture of history and hagiography, suffused with motifs from the Gospels and commonplaces from the Lives of the Saints, all amplified by the fantasies and imagination of the author.[18] In this account, the Jews kidnap William, torture, and kill him, "as if to say, 'we kill the Christian as we killed the Christ.'" The murder is thus presented not merely as a sadistic crime but as a ritual re-enactment of the crucifixion, a point necessary to buttress the claim that the child died for his faith as a Christian martyr. More than this, the murder is said to be an integral part of Jewish religious practice.

Here is the author reporting what he claims to have been told by an apostate named Theobald.

> It was laid down by [the Jews] in ancient times that every year they must sacrifice a Christian in some part of the world to the Most High God in scorn and contempt of Christ, that so they might avenge their sufferings on him . . . Wherefore the leaders and Rabbis of the Jews who dwell in Spain assemble together at Narbonne . . . and they cast lots for all the countries which the Jews inhabit; and whatever country the lot falls upon, its metropolis has to carry out the same method with the other towns and cities, and the place whose lot is drawn has to fulfill the duty imposed by authority.

Thus the earliest recorded account of Jewish ritual murder – in antiquity the accusation had been made against Christians[19] – is embellished with the suggestion of an international Jewish conspiracy, sanctioned by ancient Jewish texts, which Christians ought to fear. A chilling conclusion is placed by the author in the mouths of the "populace," which cried out "with one voice that all the Jews ought to be utterly destroyed as constant enemies of the Christian name and the Christian religion."

Such a sentence indicates that a "Final Solution" was at least conceivable in the Middle Ages. It is therefore all the more important to recall that no such program was ever articulated by a responsible spokesman of the church. More than this, where charges of ritual murder were brought to the attention of medieval popes, they regularly condemned them as baseless and inconsistent with Jewish religious teaching. One such pope perceived an underlying motive for the libel, vigorously denouncing those Christians who devise "pretexts so as to rob [the Jews] unjustly and seize their property."[20]

But here too, instructions from Rome and similar findings by secular rulers were often ignored. Once launched in England, the ritual murder charge began to appear on the continent in one city after another, clustering particularly in the German-speaking lands of central Europe. It soon entered world literature: Chaucer gave it dignity and stature in "The Prioress's Tale" at a time when there were no Jews living in England. The "Ballad of Sir Hugh or the Jew's Daughter," based on an alleged murder by Jews of Hugh of Lincoln, would be sung by Stephen Daedalus to Leopold Bloom near the end of James Joyce's *Ulysses*. In the thirteenth century, it is attested in a more familiar form: that Jews kill Christian children in order to use their blood in the observance of the Passover, a form in which it continued to appear in eastern Europe during our own century, even after the Holocaust. Despite the official repudiation of the libel by the Vatican, Simon of Trent, supposedly murdered by Jews in 1475,[21] was officially venerated by the church as a martyr until the promulgation of *Nostra aetate* in 1965.

Both the Crusader violence and the ritual murder libels originated in lower levels of Christian society and persisted despite condemnation by leading spokesmen for the church. A third major event that dramatically threatened the *modus vivendi* of centuries was initiated and executed at the pinnacles of Christian power. This was the attack against the Talmud, that massive compendium of Jewish laws and beliefs from late antiquity which became the foundation of medieval Jewish life. Launched by individuals in the twelfth century, the attack was endorsed by popes in the thirteenth, and some of them called for action.

Talmudic interpretations of biblical laws were cited as willful misreadings of the Bible, suggesting a change in the image of the Jew: rather than being the guardian of scripture and witness to its authenticity the Jew could now be presented as the malicious perverter of divine revelation. The Rabbis' imaginative, poetic musings about God were condemned as blatantly absurd, suggesting that the Jew was irrational, and therefore perhaps something less than fully human.[22] Harsh statements about Gentile idolaters were trumpeted as evidence of the Jew's misanthropic hatred of Christians. Rare references to Jesus and Mary in the Talmud were denounced as blasphemy, which no Christian authority could tolerate.

The Papal Inquisition, established in the early 1230s to combat Christian heresy, was soon investigating whether the Talmud was a heretical book. The result was a public book-burning in Paris in which all known exemplars of the Talmud in the jurisdiction of Louis IX, known as St Louis, were destroyed in a bonfire. Elegies of lament written by Jews express a grief akin to that in the wake of the Crusade massacres. Fortunately for the cause of Jewish survival, St Louis was the only European monarch to sanction such book-burning. The papacy soon reversed itself, agreeing that the Talmud, moderately censored, would be permitted to the Jews.[23]

In short, starting at the end of the eleventh century, we begin to find considerable evidence of hostility toward Jews that is quite different from the picture during the early Middle Ages. How are we to explain this fateful change? It is certainly not the case that twelfth-century Jews started behaving more reprehensibly than their eleventh-century parents, or that the average Christian suddenly became an intolerant bigot. The shifting equilibrium affecting the status of Jews was part of the powerful pressures transforming European society in the twelfth and thirteenth centuries. Yet precisely which context is most helpful in explaining the change remains a matter of scholarly debate. Four recent books, all published within the past ten years, demonstrate the multiple perspectives on the flourishing of medieval anti-Jewish sentiment.

One thesis is that medieval Christian policy toward the Jews can be understood only in the context of Christian policy toward the Muslims. According to this argument, it was the Muslims, not the Jews, who represented a real geo-political threat to medieval Christendom, and increased anti-Jewish hostility was a by-product of reactions to genuine fears of Muslim expansion. In some cases, the Jews were accused of being the actual allies of the Muslims, a fifth column insidiously paving the way for Muslim military conquest. In other cases, it was just the general association of Jews and Muslims as the only known non-Christians at the time. But either way, Jew-hatred is explained as essentially an internalized form of Muslim-hatred.[24]

A second thesis focuses on the context of the medieval church and emphasizes the ideological component as paramount. In this analysis, the decisive change was the emergence of the Mendicant orders of Franciscans and Dominicans in the thirteenth century. These new orders, which began almost immediately to provide spiritual and intellectual leadership for the church, overturned the 900-year old Augustinian doctrine of toleration and substituted a new doctrine, "one that allotted the Jews no legitimate right to exist in European society." The author does not argue that theological shifts alone were sufficient to reverse the status of the Jews, but he insists that these shifts, the work of the friars, were "a vital prerequisite, one that eventually allowed other political, social, and economic trends to take their course."[25]

A third thesis emphasizes the economic context, linking the intensification of hostility toward Jews with the shift from an economy based on exchange of services and barter to an economy based on rational financial calculation in twelfth-century Europe. As the new economic order emerged, the most innovative sectors of Christian society – merchants, bankers, professionals – were felt to be violating norms of the inherited morality, which viewed commercial activity and entrepreneur-ship with suspicion and disfavor. Resentment of the Jews developed as a projection on the part of those who saw in the Jews the same calculation for profit in which they themselves were deeply involved, without being able to justify it on religious grounds. "The main function of Jews in the Commer-cial Revolution was to bear the burden of Christian guilt for participating in activities not yet deemed morally worthy of

Christians." In short, the Jews were isolated and identified as a symbol of what the medievals considered "modernity," used as a target for the suspicions of those to whom new values were a threat.[26] This was not the last time such a pattern would emerge.

Finally, a very recent study has placed the increased hostility toward Jews in the context of treatment of other deviant groups, particularly heretics and lepers. The author argues that medieval Europe as a whole experienced a fundamental change in the twelfth century, becoming what he calls a "persecuting society," inhospitable not only to Jews but to all other deviant groups as well. Furthermore, it is maintained that persecution served not only to ward off imagined threats, but "to stimulate and assist the development of the claims and techniques of government in church and state, as well as the cohesiveness and confidence of those who operated it." In a sense, the identification of an enemy and the mobilization of forces to combat it was indispensible to the creation of the bureaucratic, efficient institutions of rule that are the legacy of the twelfth century to the modern world. In this analysis, the Jew is not so much the symbol of modernity as the challenge that makes it possible.[27]

All of this should not be taken to suggest that from 1096 on, Jewish life in medieval Europe was a series of uninterrupted persecutions.[28] In most places and at most times, ordinary Jews seemed to get along with ordinary Christians fairly well. Jewish cultural activity – biblical studies, law, philosophy, science, and mysticism – continued to flourish, often including fructifying mutual exchange with Christian neighbors. In many countries, Jewish contributions provided the impetus for economic vitality. At times Christian preachers even pointed to the Jews as providing a model worthy of emulation, in their faithful observance of the Sabbath and the holy days of the festival calendar, their abhorrence of blasphemous language, their commitment to education, and their willingness to suffer and even die for their beliefs. Jewish writers similarly identified aspects of Christian society that their co-religionists should learn from, including an exemplary intellectual life, decorous behavior in church, fervent belief and ascetic piety, and honesty in business affairs.[29]

Nevertheless, the ground rules were changing. In no single location could toleration be taken for granted. By the end of the fifteenth century, Jews had been driven out of virtually all of Western Europe: England in 1290; France in 1306 and then, after recalls, again in 1321 and 1394; Spain, home of a Jewish community at least 1000 years old and possibly dating back to the first century, in 1492. In the German lands, lacking a central power to decide for the entire realm, some ninety local urban explusions took place between 1388 and 1519.[30] In 1084, Rudiger, Bishop of Speyer, offered a charter of protection to encourage Jewish settlement, proclaiming that "I thought that the glory of our town would be augmented a thousandfold if I were to bring Jews;" in 1519, George, Bishop of Speyer, ordered a complete quarantine of Jews in his diocese, proclaiming that they were, after all "not humans, but dogs."[31] It is little wonder that when an Augustinian monk named Martin Luther initiated a movement that appeared to be shattering the foundations of the universal church, Jews thought that this must be a portent of dramatically better times. It did not take too long for some of them to conclude that even the old order was preferable.

3

The Age of the Reformation:
New Hopes and Disillusions

As everyone knows, the Reformation was one of the great turning points in the history of Christianity. Driven by forces within the Roman Catholic church, it eventually exposed the fault-lines and shattered the formal and institutional unity of Western Christendom. The church, chastened, then galvanized to militant response, would soon be confronted by a bewildering array of Protestant denominations. Like the conversion of Constantine and the First Crusade, the Reformation is an epic event which had a profound and irreversible impact upon the nature of Christian society and Christian faith.

But what is its relevance to our story? The Reformation would appear to be an exclusively internal Christian matter. The conversion of Constantine had obvious ramifications for millions of pagans in antiquity, and the Crusade was by definition a holy war against the Muslim infidel. But the Reformation pitted Christian against Christian; why should Jews be affected at all? Yet they were affected. In fact, it is remarkable how Jews and Judaism seem to lurk in the background of so many of the tensions which crystallized in sixteenth-century divisions. The Jews were certainly not on center stage, but neither were they entirely outside the theater. Their presence can be detected on two levels: first, on the level of rhetoric and second on the level of actual confrontation.

Let us consider first how those who were directly involved

perceived what was happening. We begin with the church and a region far from the center of the Reformation: the Iberian peninsula. In 1391, riots fueled by social unrest swept through Castile and Aragon with Jews as their primary victims. Given a choice of baptism or death, large numbers of Spanish Jews entered the church. After the First Crusade, those who were baptized under duress had been permitted to return to Judaism. In fourteenth- and fifteenth-century Spain they were not; the only path back to Judaism required emigration to a Muslim country. For centuries, Christian leaders had hoped for a large-scale conversion of Jews. When it occurred, as in Visigothic Spain almost eight centuries before, it brought in its wake a host of unforeseen social and religious problems.[1]

The new converts – I shall use the neutral Spanish term *conversos* – and their children and grandchildren after them, discovered that with discriminatory obstacles removed, they could advance quickly in Spanish society.[2] The traditional nobility was threatened and reacted, contemptuously dubbing the offspring of the conversos "New Christians," and later "Marranos – pigs." They also erected new legal barriers that would exclude from certain positions those who did not have the requisite *limpieza de sangre* or "purity of blood." This meant: no Jewish ancestors.

For the first time, a definition of Jewishness was legislated by which a person remained in some sense a Jew, and therefore a second-class citizen, even after baptism. This was in blatant conflict with normative Christian doctrine which held, with Paul, that baptism obliterated all prior religious distinctions, so that "there is neither Jew nor Gentile . . . in Christ" (Gal. 3:28). The church opposed and resisted the innovation, but it eventually accommodated to the powerful social pressures behind it.[3] Nineteenth-century racial anti-Semites never claimed this as a precedent, but the Spanish "purity of blood" legislation was an ominous venture into new conceptions of Jewishness.

Some members of these *converso* families continued to observe certain Jewish practices. The church considered such behavior on the part of Christians to be "Judaizing," a form of heresy. For 250 years, it had dealt with such problems through the Papal Inquisition; now in 1480 Rome, under pressure from the

27

Spanish monarchs Ferdinand and Isabella, permitted the establishment of a new Spanish Inquisition. Like its predecessor, its jurisdiction applied essentially only to Christian heretics, not to Jews.[4]

A vigorous scholarly debate rages over the nature of this institution and the challenge it faced. One school holds that those brought before the Inquisition were indeed "crypto-Jews," who pretended to be Christians out of necessity but cherished their Jewish identity and retained as much of the Jewish tradition as they could. It follows from this assumption that the Inquisition was established in response to a religious crisis of Spanish Christendom, in order to defend the purity of the faith. The other school holds that most of those denounced to the Inquisition really thought of themselves as Christians. Some of them were libelled by enemies, some of them observed certain alien practices as family folkways devoid of genuine religious significance. According to this analysis, the Inquisition was established as a political instrument to destroy the threatening class of New Christians.[5] The argument is intriguing, but for our purposes beside the point; what is important is that the church began to think of Jews not merely as stubborn dissenters, but as purveyors of Christian heresy.

This connection was made even where Jewish influence was remote. In 1415 the Council of Constance denounced John Hus, viewed by many as a precursor of the Reformation, with the words, "O cursed Judas, because you have abandoned the counsels of peace, and have counseled with the Jews, we take away from you the cup of redemption." A few years later, the theological faculty of Vienna referred to a heretical "alliance of Jews, Hussites, and Waldensians." There is no evidence for any Jewish influence on Hus or his followers; it seems more likely to be an appeal to a familiar scapegoat. But the pattern is established: where there is theological trouble, look for the Jews.[6]

This proved to be a convenient way for the Catholic church to explain the problems it was experiencing in Germany during the Lutheran Reformation. Several sources suggest the accusation that New Christian merchants traveling from Spain, known to be unreliable in their loyalty to the church and its teachings, had sewn the seeds of heresy in northern Europe.

Catholic defenders branded some of Luther's teachings, particularly his respect for the Hebrew scriptures, as heretical "Judaizing." The iconoclasts of the Reformation were denounced by Catholics as having learned from the Jews; the Lutheran "desecration" of the eucharistic sacrament was contemptuously compared with the Jewish "desecration of the Host."[7]

Perhaps the most fascinating and disturbing illustration of this charge is a forged document, which purports to be an exchange of letters between the rabbi of Arles and the leader of the Jews of Constantinople. The rabbi asks guidance for the Jews of southern France, who have been given the choice of conversion or expulsion. What should they do? The Jewish leader from Turkey allegedly responds that they should become Christians, but retain their Jewish loyalties:

> You say that you are forced to surrender your belongings: then make your children merchants, so that, little by little, they may strip the Christians of their belongings.
>
> You say that attempts are made against your lives: then make your children doctors and apothecaries, so that they may deprive Christians of their lives.
>
> You say that they are destroying your synagogues: then make your children canons and clerics, so that they may destroy their churches.[8]

Here we have not only the link between Jews and the upheavals in Christendom, but a charge of seditious conspiratorial intentionality. Whoever concocted this fictional correspondence was suggesting that the Reformation is the result of a Jewish plot to undermine Christianity from within. This sixteenth-century forgery, first published in the late nineteenth century as a text of historical interest, was quoted by anti-Semites as authentic and helped pave the path for the infamous Protocols of the Elders of Zion.

The Jews, however, turned out to be a two-edged polemical sword, used not only by the Catholics but by the Protestants as well. Luther could attack the church for its heavy-handed treatment of Jews – out of tactical rather than humanitarian considerations – charging that the established leadership had made Christianity so unappealing that Jews would have to be crazy to convert. In a passage characteristic of his rhetorical flair, he claims that "the popes, bishops, sophists, and monks have so treated the Jews that to be a good Christian one would have to become a Jew. And if I had been a Jew and had seen such idiots and blockheads ruling and teaching the Christian religion, I would rather have been a sow than a Christian."[9]

But he also turns the church's charge of contamination by Jewish influence on its head, accusing the church of being tarnished with "Jewish legalism," an excessive dependence upon structures, rules, and laws. Speaking of the Catholics, he notes that "their rules and regulations remind me of the Jews, and actually very much was borrowed from the Jews."[10] The Catholic understanding of the sacraments, he claims, is essentially the same as the Jewish view of circumcision.[11] On the crucial issue of faith versus works, Luther viewed the doctrine of the church as a variation of the Jewish error that mere acts can win favor in God's sight.

Nor was this the only negative quality shared by Catholics and Jews. When faced with an irrefutable argument from scripture, the Jews retreat to the authority of their rabbis just as Catholics fall back upon their decretals and their pope.[12] Indeed, the rabbis abuse their authority and mislead their people just as the popes have done.[13] Martin Bucer, one of Luther's most important Protestant colleagues, summed it up: "Except that the Papists venerate icons and idols and set them up for worship, while giving lip service to Christ . . . the faith and religious practices of Papists and Jews are really identical."[14]

Just as frequently, the charge of Judaizing is used by Protestants against each other. Once the orthodoxy had been successfully challenged, questions that had been settled for more than a millennium were reopened. Luther feared that Protestants of Eastern Europe had been unduly influenced by Judaism in their unitarian theology. He also suspected the Anabaptists of contamination by Judaism, accusing them of denying the New Testament sacraments of baptism and the eucharist, and of taking Old Testament social legislation with its radical implications too seriously. Informed that "Jews are making inroads" in Moravia and Bohemia, convincing Christians of the importance of circumcision and the proper observance of the Sabbath, he replied in a tract called "Against the Sabbatarians." Apparently, the renewed emphasis on scripture led some Protestants to a reconsideration of commandments central to the Old Testament, and Luther had to defend the entire movement from being besmirched by association with Jewish ways.[15]

John Calvin attacked the radical reformers for mixing politics with religion: "It is a Jewish folly to include the kingdom of Christ under the elements of this world," a charge that could be made against the Social Gospel, and liberation theologians today.[16] He also accused the Spanish theologian Michael Servetus of Judaizing in his anti-trinitarian views. As a result, Servetus was burnt at the stake in Geneva, but not before he had accused Calvin of "Jewish legalism," and "true Jewish zeal" in his commitment to the "irrational, impossible, tyrannical law" of Moses.[17] One gets the impression that throughout this tumultuous period, Judaism was a convenient and effective cudgel for beating one's religious opponents over the head. Hardly a theological development was immune from being branded as "Judaizing," and therefore heretical.[18] Nor was this mere rhetoric. Behind the charge of Judaizing was the implication of improper influence by real Jews. And it was real Jews, not just some figures in polemical rhetoric, who would bear the consequences.

How did these Jews react to the religious upheavals of the age? Let us try to imagine for a moment how Jews living in the year 1525 might have heard the reports coming from northern Europe. For more than a thousand years, the church was perceived as a monolithic antagonist which exerted enormous influence over much of the known world. Christian arguments based on proof-texts from scripture had always been countered by Jews with relative ease, and accusations of guilt for the crucifixion were generally dismissed with a shrug. But the claim that Christianity's political success on the stage of history was decisive proof of God's favor and approval, and, conversely, that defeat, subservience, humiliation proved that the Jewish people had been rejected and abandoned by God, apparently took its psychological toll.

The triumphalist argument was, after all, grounded in scripture, with its frequent linking of righteousness, divine protection, and military victory on the one hand, and of sinfulness, divine displeasure, and defeat on the other. The triumphs of Christendom, the spread of Christian faith over the entire European continent and beyond, the emergence of a great Christian civilization in the High Middle Ages with its undeniable achievements, the millennium of Christian domination, so much longer than any empire of antiquity – these were difficult for Jews to explain.

Imagine a Jew living in medieval Spain, Italy, Germany or France while the great Gothic cathedrals were being erected with their monumental sculptures and magnificent stained-glass windows, the fruit of the dedicated labors of thousands over decades, all to the glory of a rival faith. How plausible the Christian argument from success must have sounded! Now, in the early sixteenth century, that crushing argument was being undermined, as the foundations of the triumphalist church appeared to be cracking.

And what was the nature of the new challenge, which we now call the Reformation? It entailed a return to scripture as the basis of faith, including the study of Hebrew as key to the Hebrew Bible. It included a rejection of celibacy as an ideal of the religious life, and a repudiation of images and icons as objects of veneration. And this new movement was being led by a man, Martin Luther, who in 1523 published a tract criticizing the church's treatment of Jews and calling for more humane policies. That tract was entitled "That Jesus Christ was Born a Jew."

Given these perceptions of the early Reformation, it was not at all implausible for Jews to conclude that Christians were being led back on the road toward Judaism, that the new movement was part of God's plan to draw the Gentiles near to the ancestral faith. At least one Jewish author, in a suggestion strikingly similar to some of the Catholic charges (but with the opposite value judgment), saw the Lutherans as emanating from circles of Jews who had been compelled to adopt Christianity. "It seems to be divine retribution that these Jews should strike back with the weapons that were put into their hands; to punish those who compelled them to change their faith, and as a judgment upon the new faith, the Jews break out of the circle of Christian unity, and by such actions seek to reenter the road to their own faith, which they abandoned so long ago."[19] This interpretation of the dramatic events was particularly appealing to Jews of a Marrano background.

Certain Jewish thinkers went so far as to explain the unfolding developments as part of the messianic drama. God may be using Luther to bring large numbers of Gentiles to the straight path, "to accept them before the advent of the Messiah, for afterwards they are no longer acceptable."[20] As in the case of such other epic events as the Muslim Conquest, the First Crusade, and the Mongol invasion, some Jews seemed psychologically incapable of conceding that they were on the sidelines of history. Messianic speculation allowed them to think, "If you really knew God's script, you would understand that *we* are the protagonists, just as we were in ancient times." When placed in context with the fall of Constantinople in 1453, the Turkish capture of the Christian outpost of Rhodes in 1522, the invasion of Hungary by the Turks in 1526, and the sacking of Rome by German troops of the Emperor Charles V in 1527, the events of the early Reformation were understandably interpreted by Jews as a sign that the Christian era was coming to an end, that the drama of history was finally reaching its proper and just *dénouement*.[21]

Needless to say, such speculation was based on limited knowledge, strongly spiced with wishful thinking. The idea that more serious study of Hebrew scripture would bring Christians to Judaism was no more realistic than Luther's belief that a Christianity more humane and more firmly rooted in scripture would lead to wide-scale conversion by the Jews. In both cases, plausible but fundamentally fanciful expectations led to frustration, disappointment, and angry reaction. The matter came to a head with the publication in 1543 of Luther's tract, *On the Jews and Their Lies*.

It is somewhat embarrassing to discuss this work, for it is a source of pain to Lutherans and indeed to all people of good will. It is not pleasant to witness Martin Luther, who was undoubtedly a spiritual giant and a religious genius, mobilizing his powerful intellect and considerable rhetorical skill for one of the most scurrilous displays of anti-Jewish venom ever written. The Jewish religion is dismissed as less than worthless in God's sight. That God does not listen to the prayers of Jews is one of the mildest of insults.[22] Turning to an argument used by St Chrysostom, Luther insists that the commandments observed by Jews in the Diaspora have no validity because they are restricted to the land of Israel: "They cannot observe Moses' law anywhere but in Jerusalem – this they know and are forced to admit. Outside of Jerusalem they cannot have or hope to have their priesthood, kingdom, temple, sacrifices, and whatever Moses instituted for them by divine command."[23] This leads him to a mocking taunt: let the Jews return to the land of Israel and reconstitute their temple and their state; "after that is done they will soon find us on their heels, coming right after them, and we will also become Jews." But that can only occur "when God is a liar, when the devil is the truth, and when they themselves again take possession of Jerusalem."[24] Such statements reveal both a recognition of the unique bonds between the Jewish people and the land of Israel, and the lingering power of the Augustinian doctrine that Jewish misery in exile is incontrovertible testimony to the truth of Christian faith.

Even more devastating than the denigration of the Jewish religion are the attacks upon the Jews themselves, who are ferociously condemned for their alleged hatred of all Christians and their parasitical exploitation of Gentile labor. The flavor of the work can be given only by direct quotation. Jews are the "vilest whores and rogues under the sun," "full of malice, greed, envy, hatred toward one another, pride, usury, conceit and curses against us." They have been "bloodthirsty bloodhounds and murderers of all Christendom for more than 1400 years in their intentions." They are "venomous, bitter, vindictive, tricky serpents, assassins and children of the devil;" "our plague, our pestilence, and our misfortune." "It cannot be anything but the terrible wrath of God which permits anyone to sink into such abysmal, devilish, hellish, insane baseness, envy, and arrogance."[25] These, unfortunately, are not distortions removed from context; they represent the level of an onslaught sustained for well over 100 pages.

The rhetoric of abuse sometimes descends to scatalogical imagery that in many ages could not have been read aloud in polite company. The Jews "look into the devil's black, dark, lying behind and worship his stench." Do they claim to study and venerate the Bible? "You Jews are not worthy of looking at the outside of a Bible, much less of reading it. You should read only the bible that is found under the sow's tail, and eat and drink the letters that drop from there. That would be a proper bible for such prophets, who root about like sows and tear apart like swines the words of the Divine Majesty."[26] So much for the Hebrew scripture as an obvious common bond between Christians and Jews.

Nor does the hostility remain on the plane of theory. Luther defines a program of practical persecution that goes beyond any medieval policy; only the Nazis could implement and transcend it. All synagogues should be burnt to the ground and covered with dirt so that not a stone will be visible, "this in honor of our Lord and of Christendom." The homes of the Jews should be broken down and destroyed, their prayer-books and Talmuds taken away, their rabbis forbidden to teach on pain of death. Jewish economic power should be broken by withholding permission to travel, forbidding money-lending on interest, and forcing Jews to turn to manual labor.

If after all this, Christians still feel threatened, the solution is total expulsion from the realm. "For God's anger with them is so intense that gentle mercy will only tend to make them worse and worse, while sharp mercy will reform them but little. Therefore, in any case, away with them."[27] In one passage, it seems as if he is all but calling for a pogrom: "We are at fault in not avenging all this innocent blood of our Lord and of the Christians which they shed for three hundred years after the destruction of Jerusalem, and the blood of the children they have shed since then . . . We are at fault in not slaying them. Rather we allow them to live freely in our midst despite all their murdering, cursing, blaspheming, lying, and defaming."[28] Three days before his death, he expressed his final view: despite their enmity toward all Christians, "we ought to practice Christian love and beg them to convert," but "if they refuse, we should neither tolerate them nor suffer their presence in our midst."[29]

Predictably, Jews reacted with amazement,[30] abhorrence and fear. Josel of Rosheim, the unofficial leader of Germany Jewry, intuited that new ground had been broken in the teaching of contempt. This is what he wrote: "For never [before] has it been contended by any scholar that we Jews

35

ought to be treated with violence and tyranny; that no one was bound to honor any obligation toward us or keep the peace of the land where we were concerned because we decline to believe what Luther believes."³¹ This was innovation, and it was dangerous, precisely because it was recognized that Luther was not just a leader of the rabble, but a scholar of renown. In a Hebrew pun (not unsimiliar to Thomas Müntzer's reference to "Dr Luegner" [Dr Liar]), Luther's name was written as *lo tahor*, an impure man. Jews began to perceive the Reformation no longer as a movement of return to the Jewish foundations of Christianity, but as a casting off of the restraints that had safeguarded the Jews for centuries. It is, in the words of a contemporary Jewish writer, "a new faith, with all kinds of leniencies to cast off the yoke."³² Tradition was at least familiar; the abandoning of tradition was ominous, because no one could predict where it would lead.

In the context of Christian–Jewish relations, the Reformation provides an object lesson for what can happen when one group defines the other in terms of an agenda totally alien to the other group's self-definition. Each side was cast as an unwitting protagonist in the eschatological drama conceived by the other and, not surprisingly, each failed to follow the script. The result, on both sides, was bitter disillusion and increased hostility. Furthermore, the Catholic church responded to the Reformation with a militant resurgence of the most intolerant tendencies in its own tradition, and this time the Jews of Italy bore the brunt of the onslaught.

A campaign against the Talmud, similar to that of the thirteenth century, was renewed in 1553, leading once again to public book-burnings, this time in Venice and Rome, where thousands of magnificently printed volumes of the Talmud and other Jewish classics went up in flames. Victims of forced conversions in Portugal who succeeded in fleeing the Iberian peninsula had been permitted to rejoin the Jewish community in such Adriatic ports as Ancona. In 1555, the new pope Paul IV quickly withdrew the privilege ratified by his predecessor, seized all Jews who had formerly lived as Christians in Portugal, and ordered twenty-four to be burnt at the stake as heretics. Paul's program reached its climax with the promulgation that same year of the bull *Cum nimis absurdum*, formally establishing for the first time a ghetto in Rome and imposing severe discriminatory regulations. The provisions of this bull were not quite as onerous as the recommendations of Martin Luther, but the pope's ordinances were put into effect.[33]

All of this led many Jews to wonder whether there was indeed a future for Jewish life in Christendom at all. With the Ottomans welcoming Jewish refugees, one Turkish rabbi argued that no Christian country could be safe for Jews, and that Jews who settled in a Christian land rather than in the Ottoman Empire should be considered in the category of those who recklessly endanger their lives.[34] Despite these reversals, however, in the long run the impact of the Reformation was not altogether bad. At least one sixteenth-century Jew sensed that the religious wars between Catholics and Protestants, leading to a stalemated truce based on an agreement that "Every man shall worship his God according to his wish without fear," could ultimately improve the climate for Jewish life.[35] Historians agree that part of the enduring, though unexpected, legacy of the Reformation was the birth of that cluster of ideas that includes freedom of conscience, religious toleration, and the separation of church and state.[36]

When these ideas became enshrined in the institutions of democratic governments, Jews, unwittingly, were major beneficiaries. It would be no exaggeration to conclude that the Reformation, together with the Enlightenment, was thus instrumental in laying the foundations for a new kind of society in which Jews, Catholics, and various Protestant denominations could live together on an equal basis. Yet in Europe, at least, this society would have to withstand the challenge of a demonic twentieth-century ideology that would appropriate the worst elements of Luther's anti-Judaism and push them to extremes that even Luther had never imagined.

4

The Church and the Holocaust:
Dilemmas of Moral Leadership

Many sensitive Christian thinkers have argued that the Holocaust should engender a crisis of conscience for the Christian world, and I leave it to them to explore the implications of this crisis for contemporary faith.[1] My task is to address a historical question: the relationship between traditional Christian doctrines regarding the Jewish people, discussed in the previous three chapters, and the Nazi Final Solution. Should we conceive of the death camps as the final episode in the sordid history of the Christian teaching of contempt, a consummation ineluctably produced by the premises of Christian theology; or should we conceive of the Holocaust as fundamentally new, not the continuation of but the rebellion against religious tradition?

The assertion of continuity has been made by serious scholars, and it deserves to be fully explored, for the lines that link Nazi antisemitism with traditional Christian anti-Jewish teachings are by no means insignificant.[2] Let us begin where we left off, with the figure of Martin Luther. The usefulness of Luther's anti-Jewish rhetoric to the Nazis can be seen in the three twentieth-century Munich editions of Luther's *Selected Works* in German. It is no accident that *On the Jews and Their Lies* was omitted from the edition published in the 1920s and from the edition published in the late 1940s and early 1950s, but that it was published in the 1936 edition produced entirely under Nazi auspices.[3] A pamphlet containing excerpts from

Luther's work, including his program of persecution, was printed separately by the Nazis and distributed in Germany and in Sweden to support their propaganda.[4]

The renowned historian Heinrich von Treitschke is generally credited with having originated the slogan "The Jews are our misfortune" in 1879; two generations later it was taken up by the Nazis as their rallying cry. The echo of Luther is clear; he was the one who wrote that the Jews have been for 1400 years and still remain "our plague, our pestilence, and our misfortune."[5] More sinister still is Luther's comparison of the Jews in Christian society to "my gallstone, my bloody tumor, and all the other ailments and misfortunes which I have to nurse," and his statement that Christian rulers must "act like a good physician who, when gangrene has set in, proceeds without mercy to cut, saw, and burn flesh, veins, bone, and marrow." Luther is still calling for the destruction of Jewish synagogues, not of the Jews themselves. But the potentially devastating consequences of such rhetoric should be obvious. A Nazi physician in Auschwitz was asked by a Jewish doctor how he could reconcile his Hippocratic Oath with his work near the gas chambers. The Nazi physician replied, "Out of respect for human life, I would remove a gangrenous appendix from a diseased body. The Jew is the gangrenous appendix in the body of mankind."[6] Such is the power of dehumanizing rhetoric upon the human mind.

Luther himself referred to the ritual murder charge without explicitly endorsing it, but Nazi propagandists were not discouraged by this reticence. Some sixteen months after the Nazis came to power, the notorious hate-monger Julius Streicher published an issue of his mass circulation antisemitic periodical *Der Stuermer* devoted to the ritual murder theme. Under a headline stating "Jewish Murder Plan Against Gentile Humanity Exposed," a picture on the front page entitled "Victims of Jews" depicts two depraved-looking, hook-nosed Jews collecting the blood spurting from the throats of blond-haired children in a large dish.

The caption reads, "In secret rites for thousands of years, the Jew has spilled human blood. And still today the devil is persecuting us; it is up to you to clean out the hellish crew." The accompanying articles elaborate in lurid detail.[7] As late as

1943, when the majority of Poland's three million Jews had already been murdered in the death camps, Heinrich Himmler, one of the highest Nazi officials and head of the SS, wrote to a colleague urging wide circulation in Poland of stories about Jewish ritual slaughter of Christians.[8]

It may well be argued that these examples are beside the point. While Luther's denigration of Judaism was an integral part of his theology, much of his anti-Jewish rhetoric is an aberration belonging to the purview of historians and psychologists rather than theologians, and the ritual murder charge had, as we have seen, always been repudiated by responsible spokesmen for the church. They can therefore justifiably be seen as perversions of Christian doctrine exploited by Nazi propaganda, not the doctrine itself.

Our fundamental question is whether the beliefs that were for centuries central to Christian faith can be linked with the Nazi Final Solution. Does Christian theology lead directly to the murder of Jews? Did the traditional belief that Judaism was superseded make it possible for Christians to conclude that the Jew is therefore superfluous? Did the doctrine that the Jews had been rejected by God as enemies of the light help men to conceive of or to justify the death camps? Did Christians acquiesce in the Nazi Final Solution convinced that they were acting in accordance with God's will?

No historian would argue that the leading Nazis themselves were brought to their Jewish policy by traditional religious doctrines. Though Hitler once replied to two bishops who questioned the Nazi racial policy that he was only putting into effect what Christianity had preached and practiced for 2000 years, he was obviously scoring a debating point rather than explaining his own motivation.[9] Himmler insisted that the members of his SS must believe in God, for "otherwise we would be no better than the Marxists," and Hitler himself occasionally appealed to divine sanction, as in a famous passage from *Mein Kampf* where he writes: "I believe that I am acting in accordance with the will of the Almighty Creator: by defending myself against the Jew, I am fighting for the work of the Lord."[10] But the context of that passage reveals how distant is his conception of God from traditional Christian belief rooted in the Bible. The intellectual origins of Nazi antisemitism are to be found in pseudo-scientific racist and mystical-romantic-nationalist ideologies of the nineteenth century, not in the teachings of Augustine, Innocent III, or even Martin Luther.

But what about the Christian leaders who supported Hitler and his anti-Jewish policies, or at least failed to oppose them? Does their stance reveal the influence of their religious tradition, or an abandonment of it? Here is the crux of the issue. Some Christian leaders are reported to have justified the deportation to the death camps by appealing to the central Christian myth of Jewish guilt for the crucifixion. These, however, are reports, based on hearsay, not documentary evidence. Although a highly respected Jewish thinker has written that "this judgment that the Jews deserve their fate as punishment for deicide or rejecting Christ is a strong and recurrent phenomenon," I have not found clear evidence for a justification of mass murder on traditional religious grounds in anything written by a recognized leader of the church.[11]

There is, however, considerable basis for emphasizing the discontinuity between the Holocaust and traditional Christian doctrine and understanding the Final Solution as a radical break from the past.[12] For while the Nazis often gave the impression that they just wanted to turn the clock back and re-establish the medieval status of Jews, the Final Solution entailed two elements that were fundamentally new and found no support in Christian doctrine: the racial definition of the Jew, which meant that baptism was totally irrelevant in determining a Jew's status, and the commitment to mass murder of the entire Jewish population.[13]

We therefore find cases of religious leaders, both Catholic and Protestant, proclaiming the worst anti-Jewish teachings of their tradition, yet refusing to endorse Nazi antisemitism, and sometimes even using the traditional doctrine to attack Nazi policies. Dietrich Bonhoeffer, later a hero of the resistance and a martyr to the Nazis, addressed the "Jewish question" early in the Nazi regime, conceding that "the state is justified in adopting new methods" in dealing with this issue. His vision of the Jews is couched in traditional terms, buttressed by the language of Luther: "The church of Christ has never lost sight of the thought that the 'chosen people,' who nailed the redeemer of the world to the cross, must bear the curse for its action through a long history of suffering." And Martin Niemoeller, preaching on the Jews in 1937, invokes the "dark and sinister history of this people which can neither live nor die because it is under a curse which forbids it to do either," a curse imposed because "the Jews brought the Christ of God to the cross."[14]

Thus the familiar doctrine of the Jews as a reprobate people rejected and punished by God is reasserted even by those who defied the Nazi regime. By today's standards, these statements seem intolerant, reactionary, even primitive. But it is crucial to remember that the doctrine was asserted not to justify Nazi persecution but to protest against it. Bonhoeffer reiterates the Augustinian position that the Jews must be kept around as a living proof of the truth of Christian faith: "The Jew keeps open the question of Christ. He is the sign of the free mercy-choice and of the repudiating wrath of God. . . . An expulsion of the Jews from the West must therefore bring with it an expulsion of Christ."[15] Others take a step further, drawing a conclusion that appears to be totally new. In the Middle Ages, it was assumed that Christians were expected to do their part in fulfilling God's curse of the Jews; now the theological punishment is placed on a super-historical plane that excludes all human initiative.

Here is Niemoeller: "There is no charter which would empower us to supplement God's curse with our hatred. Even Cain receives God's mark, that no one may kill him; and Jesus' command, 'Love your enemies!' leaves no room for exceptions." The same point had been made a few years before in the "Bethel Confession": "*No nation* can ever be commissioned to avenge on the Jews the murder at Golgotha. 'Vengeance is *mine*, says the Lord' [Heb. 10:30]."[16] The Metropolitan Stefan of Sofia in Bulgaria is reported to have made a similar point in a sermon of September 1942. Since God has punished the Jews by exiling them from their land, it is God, not men, who determines the Jewish fate. Human beings, therefore, have no right to persecute them.[17]

For the most part, however, religious leaders who spoke out and acted on behalf of Jews did so not on the basis of traditional religious doctrine but through an appeal to standards of decency and humanity that transcend religious or ethnic differences. Some of these protests bespeak a courage, vision, and power that can hardly fail to inspire. "That children, women, fathers and mothers be treated like cattle, that members of a family be separated from one another and dispatched to an unknown destination, it has been reserved for our own time to see such a sad spectacle," wrote Monsignor Saliège, Archbishop of Toulouse, in a pastoral letter when French police in the Unoccupied Zone rounded up Jews and delivered them to the Germans for deportation. "The Jews are real men and women . . . They are part of the human species. They are our brothers."[18]

His colleague Théas, Bishop of Montauban, in his own pastoral letter, responded similarly: "I give voice to the outraged protest of Christian conscience, and I proclaim that all men, Aryans or non-Aryans, are brothers, because created by the same God; that all men, whatever their race or religion, have the right to be respected by individuals and by states."[19] In 1943, the German bishops sent out a joint pastoral letter stating, "The extermination of human beings is *per se* wrong, even if it is purportedly done in the interests of society; but it is particularly evil if it is carried out against the innocent and defenseless people of alien races or alien descent."[20]

In addition, there were many cases of extraordinary measures taken by individual Christians on behalf of Jews. One of the most celebrated examples occurred in the French village of Le Chambon sur Lignon, subject of a poignant book called *Lest Innocent Blood be Shed* and a recent documentary film entitled *Weapons of the Spirit*. Le Chambon was a stable and tightly-knit community of French Protestants, led by a pacifist pastor, André Trocmé. These Protestants, whose ancestors had been victims of persecution for centuries, opened their homes in defiance of Vichy law to Jewish refugees fleeing through the mountainous region. When the French police arrived in the summer of 1942 and demanded that all Jews be turned over, Pastor Trocmé refused. A signal had been given for the hidden Jews to be scattered through the woods; the police found only one.

A few months later, Trocmé was arrested and sent to a French concentration camp. Despite his refusal to sign an oath of obedience to all Vichy mandates, he was released, but he went into hiding for ten months when the Gestapo ordered his assassination. His cousin was not so fortunate. Arrested by the Gestapo for concealing Jewish children, he was sent to Maidanek and died in its gas chambers.[21] This small French community demonstrates the possibilities as well as the risks of popular intervention on behalf of the Jews. For understandable reasons, such heroism was the exception rather than the rule.

Examples of defiant and sacrificial courage are documented even in Poland, where the wells of Christian and popular anti-Jewish sentiment were undoubtedly the deepest. Emmanuel Ringelblum, the chronicler of the Warsaw Ghetto, reports in his diary that in December of 1940, "sermons have been preached in all the churches urging Christians to forget their misunderstandings with the Jews. On the contrary, the Jews are to be pitied because they are immured behind walls."[22] Those Jews who managed to escape the Nazis by hiding outside the ghettos survived not only because of their own ingenuity, but because Polish Christians, knowing that the punishment was summary execution or, at best, probable ostracism by their neighbors, risked their lives to help.

Some of them claim to have acted from motivations which were explicitly religious, though not in a traditional sense. A fine recent study by Nechama Tec called *When Light Pierced the Darkness* records statements made by Poles who sheltered Jews. "When I saw all the dying and dead Jews around me, then I thought that Christianity was worthless, then I became convinced that I must save whomever I could." "I am a deeply religious person and I believe that the world became so horrible, so cruel, that when we would have to account before God one would at least have to point to a few good deeds in this hell on earth. Someone had to help these persecuted Jews. And so they stayed with us." "You know how religious I am, but if Christ would stand between me and Hitler, through Christ's body I would knife him down."[23]

The following account by a survivor, then a girl of ten, reveals the sacrificial altruism that was possible even in the bleakest of times. A priest, who was concealing the Jewish girl, was beaten almost to the point of death by Germans but refused to divulge where she was. The narrative continues, "Before he died, the priest asked his housekeeper to take me out of my hiding place and bring me to him because he wanted to bless me. When she led me to him, all I saw was a pool of blood and the priest's body, torn into pieces . . . He raised his crushed and broken hand and caressed me. Once again he asked that I be hidden in a safe place, and then he died. I can't remember the priest's name. He was a parish priest in Novy-Dvor."²⁴ "I can't remember the priest's name." Surely one of the most poignant sentences in the literature of the Holocaust, a sentence suggesting how much of the full account of heroic, anonymous defiance has been lost beyond recovery.

The behavior of the highest levels of church leadership was often somewhat less inspiring. During the Middle Ages, anti-Jewish agitation instigated among the lower clergy was often criticized by the popes. During the Nazi era, the situation was reversed: ordinary clergy frequently showed greater willingness to resist the Final Solution than did the princes of the church. In July 1933, six months after Hitler came to power – six months of severe repression that transformed Germany from a parliamentary democracy into a one-party totalitarian state – the Vatican ratified a concordat with the Nazi regime. It had been negotiated by Cardinal Secretary of State Pacelli, formerly papal nuncio in Berlin, later to become Pope Pius XII. The church pledged non-interference in political matters and agreed that new bishops would take an oath of loyalty to the government; in return it was promised the right to continue its religious and educational programs.

Reporting to his cabinet, Hitler described the concordat with the Vatican as a diplomatic triumph "in the uncompromising struggle against international Judaism," giving badly needed prestige abroad to his regime and undermining the possibility of Catholic resistance at home.²⁵ He had no intentions of abiding by its fine print, and he began to violate its provisions almost immediately. But like those German Army officers who had sworn an oath of personal loyalty to the Führer, the Vatican treated its undertaking as an absolutely binding commitment which no behavior on the part of the Nazis could negate.

Displeasure with the Nazi regime – though not with its antisemitic legislation – was expressed in an encyclical by Pope Pius XI in 1937. German bishops played a leading role in attacking Hitler's program of "euthanasia" for the "incurably insane," and their public opposition to the program was a major factor leading to its discontinuance.[26] But the Vatican policy with regard to the Final Solution was one of public silence at the top, a refusal to endorse any course of action that would threaten the Vatican's neutrality in the war or violate the 1933 concordat, giving latitude to local bishops to determine their behavior in accordance with local conditions, and working "behind the scenes" for individual acts of humanitarian rescue. Three papal nuncios, in Rumania, Slovakia, and Hungary, intervened with the governments of these largely Catholic countries on behalf of the Jews, with notable success.

By contrast, the Nazi sympathies of the nuncio in Berlin, Archbishop Cesare Orsenigo, were notorious even at the time. In September 1941 he warned the Vatican that any approach to the German authorities on behalf of the Jews, even those who were baptized, might stir up the already deep antisemitism of the authorities – this at a time when plans for the death camps were being vigorously developed. In July 1942 he informed his colleagues in Rome that there was no point in asking about deported Jews; there was no trace of them, and it was "inadvisable to interest oneself in them."[27] The refusal of this papal nuncio to meet with Kurt Gerstein, an SS officer who tried to communicate his eye-witness account of the Polish death camps, was dramatized in the first scene of Rolf Hochhuth's controversial play *The Deputy*.

The Vatican's Secretary of State, Luigi Cardinal Maglione, had access both to detailed information about the deportations and appeals for concrete measures. One example came in March 1943, when Jewish leaders asked the Vatican to intervene with the President of predominately Catholic Slovakia to permit 1000 children to emigrate and settle in Palestine, a plan to which the British had consented. Internal documents reveal the reasons for Maglione's denial of the request: appealing to the long opposition by the Vatican to a Jewish homeland in Palestine, he asserted that the Holy Land was more sacred to Catholics than to Jews and that Catholics would justifiably fear for their rights if Jews ever became a majority.[28] Implication: the Vatican could not support the saving of 1000 Slovakian Jewish children because it might threaten the rights of Catholics living in Palestine.

In October 1943, at the time of the mass arrests of Jews in Rome, leading to a major deportation – the first time in 1900 years that Jews had been expelled from Rome – Cardinal Maglione protested privately to the German ambassador and hinted at the possibility of a public protest. But he agreed to the ambassador's request that the content of their conversation not be reported to Berlin.[29] Of the more than 1000 Jews who were deported, only fifteen are known to have survived the war.

The most vigorous debate focuses on the figure of Pope Pius XII.[30] His only public statement came in the Pope's Christmas message of 1942. By this time, most of the Jews of Poland and the USSR had already been murdered, either by special machine-gun units or by gassing in death camps. These facts were known in the West. Yet substantial Jewish communities remained, threatened with deportation. On 17 December, the United States, Great Britain, and the USSR joined in a Three Power Declaration, unambiguously proclaiming to the world that Hitler's intention to exterminate the Jewish people in Europe was now being put into effect and threatening punishment after the war for those involved. Then it was the Pope's turn.

The only reference to what we now call the Holocaust came near the end of his forty-five minute speech, when the Pope mentioned "the hundreds of thousands of persons who, without any fault on their part, sometimes only because of nationality or race, have been consigned to death or to a slow decline." The vagueness in the formulation, avoiding any mention of Jews as victims or Nazis as perpetrators, was intentional. When President Roosevelt's special representative pleaded with the Pope for a more forthright statement, the reply was that he "could not name the Nazis without at the same time mentioning the Bolsheviks."[31] Even-handedness won the day. In July 1943 the Pope wrote to the Bishop of Berlin that: "At the present time, the only direct aid I can give [the victims of German persecution] is through prayer, but the time will come when circumstances will once more permit my voice to be raised in their favor."[32] If that time ever did come, it was by then too late.

The role of the historian is to recover and present the "facts," to explain and interpret why people acted the way they did, not to sit in judgment over their decisions. Yet the issue of Christian responsibility for the Holocaust, focused particularly upon the leadership of the Catholic church, has now become part of the historical legacy of contemporary Christian–Jewish relations, and it is therefore necessary to move beyond pure history at least to frame the questions that any value judgment might entail.

First, there is the question of fairness. The Catholic church is, among other things, a political entity, in some ways more analogous to a sovereign state than to a religious denomination. Is it perhaps misguided to assume that any state has an obligation of humanitarian intervention on behalf of an oppressed group for which it bears no legal responsibility, particularly if such intervention entails definite risks?[33] That the church has a responsibility for the well-being of its own members is beyond question, and this would include those Jews who had been baptized as Roman Catholics. But why should the church be held accountable for alleged failures to act more vigorously on behalf of the masses of European Jews who remained Jews and – if the truth be told – probably harbored a certain contempt for the church and all that it represented? Is the underlying premise of the critique valid and appropriate?

Whether or not the modern nation-state has a moral responsibility to take risks and make sacrifices on behalf of the suffering beyond its borders is open to debate. But the church claims to be not merely a state but a unique religious and moral force. Its position on abortion provides a useful analogy. Starting from the axiom that the fetus is a human being, the church claims a responsibility to act on behalf of *all* fetuses, regardless of the religious affiliation of the parents. By its own claim, it must actively oppose the murder of any innocent human beings, not just Roman Catholics. The issue therefore is not whether an unfair and unrealistic expectation is being imposed, but whether during this critical period the church lived up to its own standards.[34]

A second question is more pragmatic. Would a concerted movement of protest by leaders of the church have helped? The Nazis ruthlessly suppressed all forms of active resistance and pursued their goal of destroying the Jews of Europe with single-minded intent. Some protests backfired. An example frequently cited by defenders of the Vatican is the public protest of Dutch bishops in July 1942 against the deportation of Dutch Jews from the Netherlands. The Nazi official in command, angered not so much by the protest addressed to him as by the bishops' decision to incorporate it into a pastoral letter, responded by ordering the arrest and deportation of Jewish converts to Catholicism, including those in monasteries and convents.[35] (Among those deported to their death was the Carmelite nun, Dr Edith Stein, known as Sister Theresia Benedicta, who in April 1933 had written to the Vatican expressing concern over German antisemitism. The beatification of Sister Theresia as a Christian martyr in 1987 was deemed offensive by some who insisted that the Nazis murdered her not as a Christian but as a Jew.)

Yet the same example of the Dutch bishops can be used to show the Nazi sensitivity to such protests. There is considerable evidence that the Nazis were not impervious to clear expressions of public opinion, either in Germany or elsewhere in Europe, and many believe that coordinated open confrontation by the church would have had an effect. Provost Heinrich Grueber, who was himself arrested and beaten by the Nazis, speaking after the war in retrospect, noted that Nazi leaders were reluctant to arrest German bishops. "If on a Sunday, all the bishops in Germany had appeared in their pulpits with Jewish stars pinned to their vestments in place of their gold and silver crosses, that would have been act understood not only by the persecuted Jews, but by all the faithful in Germany and elsewhere."[36] An Italian correspondent who asked the Pope why there was no clear protest reports the papal reply, "Dear friend, do not forget that millions of Catholics serve in the German armies. Shall I bring them into conflicts of conscience?"[37] That is precisely the effect that many would have wished.

What if the Pope had in December 1942 unambiguously condemned the Nazi annihilation of the Jews and threatened with excommunication any Catholic who abetted this program? What if the Pope had in October 1943 called upon Italian Catholics, in the spirit of Christian martyrdom, to join him in reporting for deportation to wherever the Jews of Rome were being sent? Would this have led to a German seizure of the Vatican and the imposition of a Nazi pope? Or would it have forced the Nazis to back down before a wave of mass indignation, as they did in other places?

Did the Vatican behave too much as a political institution in these critical times, rather than as a force of moral vision? Should religious leaders have done what they knew to be right whether or not they believed their actions would be efficacious? Do those who were not faced by the nightmarish realities of Nazi power have the right to expect that any other human being, even a religious leader, should have been prepared for martyrdom? These are questions which may never have definitive answers. But their legacy remains as an irritant and challenge for Jewish–Christian understanding to this day.

5

Burdens from the Past,
Opportunities for the Future

In the opening chapter, I identified four issues in the early
church which had powerful repercussions in the history of
Christian–Jewish relations – issues pertaining to the Christian
definition of identity, scripture, sacred space, and the bound-
aries of toleration. In assessing the legacy of the past and its
impact upon the opportunities for contemporary dialogue and
mutual understanding, I shall return to these four issues,
considering them in reverse order.

We have seen that for many centuries, the fundamental
doctrine controlling the church's position on the toleration of
Jews was articulated by St Augustine: the Jews bear God's
curse because of their rejection of the Christ, but they must be
permitted to live alongside Christians so that their degradation
will serve as a constant reminder of the consequences of sin.
The two aspects of this doctrine were reasserted throughout the
Middle Ages: on the one hand, Jews should not be permitted to
flourish; on the other, they should not be put to death. Even
during the period of the Holocaust, Christian thinkers appealed to this doctrine, often to oppose the Nazi policies.

The most plausible alternative to this doctrine in the Middle
Ages was never that Jews should be allowed to live as equals
with Christians, but rather that Jews should either accept
Christianity or be expelled from Christian lands. After the
Holocaust, however, both the Augustinian doctrine and its
historical alternative have been repudiated. Leaders of the

Catholic church at Vatican II wrought a silent revolution when they said in *Nostra aetate* (1965) that "Jews should not be presented as rejected or accursed by God, as if this followed from the Holy Scriptures."[1]

The implications of this statement were further elaborated in the Vatican's 1985 "Notes on the correct way to present the Jews and Judaism in preaching and catechesis in the Roman Catholic Church:" "We must in any case rid ourselves of the traditional idea of a people punished, preserved as a living argument for Christian apologetic. It remains a chosen people." This was not, of course, just a "traditional idea;" it was established doctrine, formulated by the most profound of the church fathers, reiterated by popes over many centuries. Its formal abandonment clears the way for a totally new conceptualization of the church's relationship with the Jewish people.

Protestant groups have also rejected the old theological model in favor of a new one. In 1968, a World Council of Churches report characterized Jewish historical experience not as proof of the dismal fate of the Christ-killer, but as "a living and visible sign of God's faithfulness to men." The statement explicitly rejects "any thought of considering their sufferings during the ages as a proof of any special guilt." This same statement recognizes that Christians had a hand in much of Jewish suffering, confessing "the guilt of Christians who have all too often stood on the side of the persecutors instead of the persecuted."[2] The final step, an affirmation that not only Christians but Christian doctrine has led to persecution of the Jews, is taken in a document "commended to the churches for study and action" by the Executive Committee of the WCC in 1982: "Teachings of contempt for Jews and Judaism in certain Christian traditions proved a spawning ground for the evil of the Nazi Holocaust."[3]

Various denominations have articulated similar ideas. A 1969 committee report of the Lutheran World Federation, expressing anguish over the "deep and tragic involvement of men of Christian tradition in the persecution of the Jewish people," called particular attention to "the cruel and dangerous anti-Jewish attacks in some of the writings of the old Luther."[4] In 1987, the Presbyterian Church (USA) in a provisional statement on Christian–Jewish relations acknowledged "in repentance the church's long and deep complicity in the proliferation of anti-Jewish attitudes and actions through its 'teaching of contempt' for the Jews," noting in its explication that this teaching was "a major ingredient that made possible the monstrous policy of annihilation of Jews by Nazi Germany." Similarly, the United Church of Christ in a 1987 statement affirms that "the Church's frequent portrayal of the Jews as blind, recalcitrant, evil, and rejected by God . . . has been a factor in the shaping of anti-Jewish attitudes of societies and the policies of governments. The most devastating lethal metastasis of this process occurred in our own century during the Holocaust."[5]

Such statements move beyond any position taken by the Catholic church. While the Vatican has repudiated the portrayal of Jews as "rejected or accursed by God" and has condemned all expressions of antisemitisim, it has not, so far as I can tell, drawn a direct connection between traditional church doctrine and anti-Jewish behavior, or admitted that representatives of the church sometimes served as purveyors or instruments of persecution. It has pointedly refused to recognize any possible link between the teaching of contempt and the Holocaust, asserted in the Protestant statements above.

In a moving and powerful statement about the Holocaust made by Pope John Paul II in August of 1987, precisely the opposite lesson is drawn: "Reflection upon the *Shoah* shows us to what terrible consequences the lack of faith in God and a contempt for man created in his image can lead."[6] As for the policy and behavior of the church during the Nazi period, there appears to be little expression of self-criticism at the top. When the storm of controversy erupted over Rolf Hochhuth's play *The Deputy*, Catholic spokesmen not surprisingly rallied to the defense of Pope Pius XII on historical and moral grounds.

Where does this leave us today? I hope to have shown that both questions – the role of traditional Christian doctrine and the policy of the Vatican – are extremely complex. Where carefully nuanced formulations are required, polemical and blatantly inaccurate accusations – such as "the church did nothing" – often prevail. Where the facts leave room for legitimate difference of interpretation, particularly regarding

the subtle interplay of varying motivations, polarization sometimes wins the day. It might be argued that Jewish spokesmen
have occasionally shown insufficient sensitivity to the effect of
attacks upon the character of either the current pope or one
who is still remembered and revered by millions of Roman
Catholics. There is also an unfortunate tendency to use the
brush too broadly in painting a picture of guilt. *Nostra aetate*,
reversing a tradition almost as old as Christianity itself,
proclaimed that responsibility for the crucifixion "cannot be
charged against all the Jews, without distinction, then alive,
nor against the Jews of today."[7] Does not the same principle
apply to the responsibility of Christians for the Holocaust?

Nor have Catholic spokesmen always been conscious of
Jewish sensibilities in making their case. Here is an example,
written by a French writer, Jacques Gommy.

> What was there, then, for Pius XII to do? He had warned
> that the unspeakable horrors of technological warfare could
> destroy the world. No one listened. Pius XII, consequently,
> denounced all atrocities, all, including the extermination of
> the Jews, though he could not condemn only one side when
> both were equally guilty. In addition, Pius XII did what the
> West did not in the Hungarian situation, he acted. He did
> everything in his power to stop human suffering and to save
> human lives, that is, he did far more than anyone else did.
> And though in this world we tend to ignore the power of
> prayer, surely his constant prayers and fatherly concern for
> all mankind touched the infinite mercy of God and helped
> bring an end to the homicidal folly. Surely that counted
> above all.[8]

I will pass by the outright falsification of history in the
assertion that only the Pope acted in "the Hungarian situation"
– as if Raul Wallenberg, working for the US War Refugee
Board with the cooperation of the Swedish government, never
existed! Look at the other statements: the Pope "did more than
anyone else" to stop human suffering. And his constant prayers
surely "touched the infinite mercy of God" and helped end the
Holocaust. From a traditionalist Catholic perspective, I
suppose this is comprehensible, but think of how it sounds to
Jews. The prayers of six million Jewish victims apparently

could not move God to halt the bloodbath, but the prayers of the Pope did? A contemporary Jewish thinker has suggested the following working principle for legitimate discourse about the Holocaust: "No statement, theological or otherwise, should be made that would not be credible in the presence of the burning children."9 In my judgment, this particular defense of Pope Pius XII fails dismally by that standard.

A second major question related to the land. The contemporary state of Israel is invariably the subject on which feelings run hottest in inter-faith conferences. On the Jewish side, there used to be a fairly straightforward reality. The experiences of 1948, 1967, and 1973 made Israel a simple touchstone in the minds of most American Jews. While the Jewish people and religion were able to survive almost 1900 years in exile, without a state of their own, the loss of Israel today, so soon after the Holocaust, would be a trauma from which the entire people might never recover. Any religious group that could not recognize the right of Jews to sovereignty over one tiny portion of the earth's surface, or support the threatened state when Egyptian armies mobilized on its borders and tried to sever its economic jugular vein at Sharm a-Sheikh, or when Egypt and Syria initiated a massive surprise attack on Yom Kippur, did not seem to be an appropriate partner for authentic dialogue. If you hesitate and waver over my brother's right to survive, what is there to discuss?

The summer and early fall of 1982 produced a new equation. For the first time, Jews in Israel and in America were deeply ambivalent or sharply divided over the wisdom of policies and actions taken by the Israeli government. These internal divisions intensified with the cycle of violence and repression beginning in December of 1987 and called by Palestinian Arabs "the uprising." Yet there appears to be little erosion of the underlying commitment felt by American Jews to the secure survival of Israel, and little dissent that Israel's welfare remains near the top of any authentic Jewish agenda. It is against this background that we need to evaluate the stance of the various Christian groups. I will divide them into three.

The position of the Catholic church has changed dramatically in theory, considerably less in practice. At the beginning of the century, the church's approach to the idea of a

Jewish return to the land of Israel was based on traditional theological foundations. This is clearly demonstrated by the remarks of Pope Pius X in an audience with Theodor Herzl, the leader of the Zionist movement, held on 25 January 1904. The Pope's statements are recorded in Herzl's diary:

> We are unable to favor this movement . . The ground of Jerusalem, if it were not always sacred, has been sanctified by the life of Christ . . . The Jews have not recognized our Lord, therefore we cannot recognize the Jewish people . . . It is disagreeable to see the Turks in possession of our Holy Places. We simply have to put up with it. But to sanction the Jewish wish to occupy these sites, that we cannot do . . . Either the Jews will retain their ancient faith and continue to await the Messiah whom we believe has already appeared – in which case they are denying the divinity of Jesus and we cannot assist them. Or else they will go there with no religion whatever, and then we can have nothing at all to do with them.[10]

According to this account, all of the assumptions of the traditional triumphalist theology are in place. It is the life of Christ that sanctifies the soil of Jerusalem. A Jewish people that either remains traditionally Jewish or becomes secular has no right to return to its ancient homeland. That would violate the doctrine that the Jews must remain scattered and homeless as punishment for their heinous sins. Only when the Jews recognize the true Messiah, who has already come, will they be entitled to a share in the holy land. Until that time, the church can tolerate Turkish control of the holy places, but it cannot approve of a Jewish national return. Herzl reports that the Pope concluded, if a refuge from persecution is needed, let them go anywhere else.

The theological foundations of this negative stance have been abandoned by the church in Vatican II. Yet the church still refuses to extend formal recognition to the state of Israel, and this remains a constant irritant.[11] Various explanations have been given: the Vatican has many interests and agenda items beyond its relationship with world Jewry; it must weigh political considerations such as a fear of retaliation by Arab countries against small Christian minorities in their midst, and the influence of a Catholic Palestinian lobby committed to Palestinian rights. Indeed, in August of 1987, the Vatican stated explicitly that the obstacles to the formal recognition of Israel were not theological but political – apparently implying that if the theological problems have been overcome, the political problems may be easier. Jews hear these explanations as plausible, knowing that Israel does not need the church's approval of its legitimacy.

To many Jews, however, the *status quo* is still not fully comprehensible. There are some issues of such symbolic importance that they should transcend mundane political calculations. Pope John Paul II's visit to the Great Synagogue of Rome in April of 1986 was a dramatic gesture of respect for the dignity of the Jewish religion. But most Jews today consider the state of Israel to be an integral component of Jewish dignity and survival. Despite protestations to the contrary, something of the attitude expressed by Pius X seems to linger: it is tolerable if Muslims exercise sovereignty over Christian holy places – that is a geo-political fact which even the popes who called for Crusades could begrudgingly accept – but for Jewish soldiers to ensure security at the Church of the Holy Sepulchre – that the church can never endorse. So long as the Vatican refrains from extending full diplomatic recognition to Israel, including full ambassadorial exchange, many Jews will remain unconvinced that the legacy of medieval triumphalist theology is really dead.

American Protestantism divides into two quite different groups on this issue. The most powerful, unquestioning political and economic support for the state and government of Israel comes from the Evangelicals.[12] Particularly at times when Israel is beleaguered and embattled, Jews recognize this and appreciate it. Yet Jews feel considerable ambivalence about the Evangelical position. They remain distrustful of Evangelical motives in their support of Israel, and they fear that to welcome this support while ignoring the eschatological belief-structure undergirding it may be either cynical or naive.

Many Jews suspect that Evangelicals are concerned not about Israel as a reality, but about Israel as a doctrine. The Holy Land tours, which bring tens of thousands of Evangelical pilgrims each year, are of immense economic value to Israel.

57

But when they are limited to the Sea of Galilee, the Church of the Nativity, and the old City of Jerusalem, overlooking all that the Jewish people has accomplished in that land during the past 100 years, is it truly Israel that they are seeing? Finally, at a time when there is considerable dissent both in Israel itself and within American Jewry about policies taken by the Israeli government, the uncritical support of hawkish positions expressed by some Evangelicals, often because of their understanding of eschatological doctrine, is not perceived by all Jews as helpful. All these are issues that deserve to be more fully explored.

On the other hand, Jews share with the mainline and liberal Protestant denominations a legacy of cooperation and communication. Before Vatican II, these groups were the only Christians interested in dialogue. They are unambiguously committed to the principle of religious pluralism in America, and they have forged with Jews the agenda on a wide range of critical social issues. Today they are the most open to healthy dialogue based on mutual respect. But they have serious problems with many of Israel's policies, and their outspoken criticism strikes many Jews as hypocritical and unfair.

Sentiments expressed by Henry Siegman some years ago about a figure from the Catholic radical left seem even more apropos of some liberal Protestant critics: they are "nourished by a Christian universalism which cannot abide the earthiness of Jewish particularism. They love Jews who are disincarnated, who are suffering servants, who are ghostly emissaries and symbols of an obscure mission. They cannot abide Jews who are flesh-and-blood people, who are men and women like other men and women in all their angularities and specificities, who need to occupy physical space in a real world before they fulfill whatever loftier aspirations they may have. They are distressed by the notion that Jews should want a flesh-and-blood existence as a people in the real geography of this world."[13]

Few would suggest that any criticism of Israel from Christian sources necessarily reflects an antisemitic bias. There is, however, a fundamental difference between criticism from within and criticism from without. The prophets held ancient Israel to a higher standard of morality than the surrounding nations out of a love for their people that was evident throughout their careers. When the church fathers quoted the prophets out of context to prove to the world the reprobate character of the Jews, their motives were perverse, and the impact of their criticism was potentially devastating.

The same words, when repeated outside the context of underlying commitment, may sound quite different – not the anguished reproach of a lover's quarrel, but the mean-spirited, self-serving attack of those who seek any excuse to embarrass the one whom you treasure. When criticism of particular policies comes from Christians who have established their credentials as supporters and lovers of Israel, not only for its role in some eschatological scheme but for its own sake, Jews can generally accept it as appropriate and legitimate. When it comes from Christians whose underlying position on Israel has always been suspect, the very same words sometimes sound grating and smug.[14]

I will touch upon the final two issues more briefly. We recall that relatively early in its history, the church decided that the Hebrew Bible would remain part of its sacred scripture, and that it would thus in effect share a scripture with the Jewish people. I have argued that the Gnostic alternative might have made the demonizing of the Jewish people even easier for Christians. A common text at least established the possibility of a common ground for communication. Occasionally this produced mutually beneficial common scholarship; more often it led to sterile argumentation.

What about today?[15] Though one frequently hears the assertion that Christians share with Jews a profound commitment to the Bible as the Word of God, a cautionary note is in order. We must not forget that the Hebrew Bible is not the same as the Christian Old Testament, even though it may contain precisely the same books. The old stereotyped Christian reading of scripture still lingers, contrasting the vengeful, zealous God of the Old Testament with the merciful, loving, gracious God of the New.[16] This is certainly not an image Jews would recognize as authentic.

Furthermore, the essential story of the Hebrew Bible as read by Jews is quite different from that of the Old Testament as read by most Christians. For Jews, it is essentially a book of history and of law, providing an account of a people's origin and golden age and the constitution of its legal system. For Christians, it is essentially a book of prophecies and types, a preparation for things to come, important not as history in its own right but as prefigurement and prophecy of a new dispensation which would make the old obsolete. Reading the same words, the content turns out to be quite different.

Often, we do not even read the same words. For the Jew, the Bible is always the Hebrew text. While Judaism has never forbidden translation, as did Islam, and for some time and for very different reasons the Catholic church, no serious Jewish study of the Bible has ever been separated from the original Hebrew. By contrast, one frequently hears Christians, particularly of the more fundamentalist orientations, quoting "God's Word" as if the text was originally uttered or revealed in King James English. We should not forget that when we quote an English verse, we are not quoting the Bible; we are merely quoting one translation of the Bible.

This point is not mere academic pedantry. Translation always entails difficult and sometimes arbitrary decisions. A word or phrase in one language often has two possible meanings; the translator must usually render one at the expense of the other. What begins as multivalent and suggestive ambiguity emerges in translation as straightforward simplicity. This is especially pronounced in translation from biblical Hebrew, which has no punctuation, no indications where a quotation ends, hundreds of verbs with unclear subjects and pronouns with unclear referents, an imperfect tense that can mean you must, you may, or you will, and that omnipresent *vav* conversive, which can have at least half a dozen different meanings.

For the Jew, therefore, the Bible, read and studied in Hebrew, is a very different kind of text from that quoted in English. It is fraught with ambiguities and obscurities, forever inspiring new and legitimate interpretations, an open-ended text the meaning of which may be ultimately elusive, which one is left to wrestle with and probe. We are not certain how to translate properly even the first sentence of the book of Genesis. This may be why in theological matters Jews have traditionally had such a marked tolerance for diversity.

Where the Jewish community has tried to impose a measure of conformity upon its members, and this is primarily in the realm of behavior governed by Jewish law, the Bible has been understood and applied through a tradition of rabbinic interpretation. There is no model in traditional Jewish life for appealing directly to the Bible as a source of authority over others. *Sola Scriptura* is not a live option in the Jewish context, any more than the US Supreme Court today could decide to throw out all the judicial decisions of the past 200 years and adjudicate each case solely on their direct reading of the Constitution. For the traditional Jew, the meaning of the Bible is largely open-ended, but the Bible functions as it has been understood by the rabbis over the past 2000 years. All of this is quite different from the Christian Bible, particularly that of the Protestants.

The final issue, which goes back to the very beginnings of the Christian church, pertains to identity and lines of demarcation. The decision made by what became the normative church was that one did not have to be a Jew to be Christian, and that the major thrust of evangelistic energy would be directed toward the Gentile world. Jews would be permitted to live as Jews, and not baptized under duress, but the conversion of Jews, both as individuals and as an entire people, would remain throughout the centuries as a paramount Christian aspiration and goal.

Perhaps second only to modern Israel, the question of Christian mission to the Jews is today the most vehemently debated in internal Christian circles. Some Christians, particularly Evangelicals, feel unable to compromise on a supersessionist theology which holds that Christianity has taken the place of Judaism. As one spokesman has put it: "We evangelicals maintain that by the whole Christ-event Judaism *qua* religion has been superseded, its propaedeutic purpose accomplished. Since the Messiah has come and offered his culminating sacrifice, there is, as we see it, no temple, no priesthood, no altar, no atonement, no forgiveness, no salvation, and no eternal hope in Judaism as a religion."[17] If that is the starting point, it is obvious that a mission to the Jews remains important; indeed, a renunciation of such a mission would be to abandon Jews to eternal despair.

Other denominations have explicitly abandoned the supersessionist model.[18] The Presbyterians in 1987 stated that "Christians have not replaced Jews." Jews are "already in a covenantal relationship with God," and remain with Christians "partners in waiting." In the same year, the United Church of Christ affirmed that "Judaism has not been superseded by Christianity; . . . Christianity is not to be understood as the successor religion to Judaism; God's covenant with the Jewish people has not been abrogated."[19] Yet some of those who could support such statements still feel bound by the Gospel's challenge to bring the "good news" to the entire world and believe that excluding in principle the Jewish people from their witness would be a violation of their responsibility and self-understanding as Christians.[20]

Jewish antipathy toward Christian proselytizing among Jews is powerful and deep. Whether such proselytizing results in a formal severing of all links with the Jewish community or in the dual identity model espoused by "Messianic Jews," "Jews for Jesus," "Hebrew Christians," or any of the other half-dozen names by which such groups are known, the consensus ranging from ultra-orthodox to secular Jews is that the Christian mission must be resisted at all costs.

How might this consensus be explained? Historical memory can be a strong force for an ancient people. It is impossible to eradicate the psychic legacy of sixteen centuries in which Christians, often backed by the power of the state, exerted various kinds of pressure upon Jews to renounce their "blindness" and accept the "true faith," the legacy of generations of Jews who could have made things so much easier for themselves by succumbing to these pressures, yet refused, sometimes at the cost of their lives. Too much has happened in the relationship between the two communities over the centuries for Jews to consider dispassionately the merits of conversion or even of a compromise version that would somehow have the best of both worlds. 1900 years ago, Jewish Christianity may have been a real option; from the Jewish perspective, history has long since rendered it obsolete.

Secondly, the Jewish people today is fighting a demographic battle for its survival. There are still fewer Jews in the world today than there were in 1939. Statistics about reproduction rates, average age, intermarriage, lead many to conclude that the number of Jews in the world will decline significantly over the next few generations. The very existence of a Jewish people

100 years from now is an agonizing question-mark. In such circumstances, the Jewish community simply cannot afford a hemorrhaging to other faith-groups.

In some ways, the claims of the "Jews for Jesus" that their Jewish identity is fulfilled by accepting a messiah who has already come, though in practice they espouse a rather high christology and an agenda of concerns that hardly reflects that of American Jewry, seem even more insidious.[21] Few would question the right of these individuals to find their own religious way, or the right of the Christians to count them among their own. But those who use traditional Jewish rituals and *sancta* in affirming Jesus as their savior are not a basis of commonality between Christians and Jews; they are an irritating source of friction.

More complicated is the question whether Jews will insist that a Christian commitment to a universal mission is incompatible with dialogue, destined to produce suspicion and distrust. One of the universally accepted ground rules of dialogue requires that each side recognize the right of the other to define itself in its own terms. How are Jews to respond when they are told that a universal mission is an inherent part of the self-definition of the Christians to whom they are speaking? Do they have the right to argue that a history of persecution requires contemporary Christians to abandon this religious principle as a sign of good will, a pre-condition for communication? This is an issue on which Jews themselves remains divided.[22]

"History is a nightmare from which I am trying to awake," said Stephen Daedalus to a colleague in *Ulysses*. Though not quite as much as is often assumed, there is much in the history of Jewish–Christian relations that might justify the profound pessimism of this sentiment. But the purpose of this review is not to relive the nightmare, and certainly not to foster feelings either of guilt among the descendants of the persecutors or of self-righteousness among the descendants of the victims. Rather it is to suggest some corrections to prevalent misconceptions about the historical record and some lessons that might be learned from the past: that the marriage of religion and political power often produces the ugly offspring of intolerance and persecution; that the line between faithful devotion and exclusivist fanaticism can be deceptively thin; that *any* group which believes that it alone knows God's will or that it alone carries God's banner risks perverting God's purpose.

Having wrestled with these lessons and clarified for each other what it is that gives us pain,[23] Jews and Christians can begin to build on a more solid foundation an alliance for a common agenda of action in causes that require concerted effort by all people of good will: an alliance to ensure that human folly and greed will never destroy God's creation through nuclear catastrophe or a poisoning of our physical environment; to end once and for all the scandals of homelessness and hunger in an affluent society; to pursue the elusive goals of social justice and equal opportunity for every one of God's children; to affirm the claims of faith and the ideals of stewardship and accountability before the corrosive challenge of a militantly secular, hedonistic, self-indulgently acquisitive worldview.

Whether because of the vagaries of historical circumstance, the limitations of human understanding and imagination, or the mysteries of divine providence, Jews and Christians have walked widely divergent paths for 1900 years. No one would suggest that the paths can or even should be united today, but perhaps we can ensure that they will lead us in the same direction.

Notes

1. Jews and Christians in Antiquity

1. See Acts 15:1; this group has been called, somewhat flippantly, the "circumcision party" (Rosemary Ruether, *Faith and Fratricide*, New York 1974, 82). The resistance to Paul on this issue is discussed in every history of early Christianity, although the formulation is usually quite different from mine. Cf., e.g., Martin Hengel, *Acts and the History of Earliest Christianity*, London and Philadelphia 1979, 92–110.

2. Justin Martyr, *Dialogue with Trypho*, 47.1–4. The passage is included in J. Stevenson (ed.), *A New Eusebius*, London 1968, 68–9. See Theodore Stylianopolous, *Justin Martyr and the Mosaic Law*, Missoula, Montana 1975, 34–5.

3. Jerome wrote that if Jewish converts to Christianity "are allowed to observe in the churches of Christ what they have initiated in the synagogues of Satan, I will tell you my view – they will not become Christians, they will make us Jews!" Augustine expressed his agreement that "the ceremonies of the Jews are both baneful and deadly to Christians and that whoever keeps them, whether Jew or Gentile, is doomed to the abyss of the devil." See the discussion of this exchange by John Gager, *The Origin of Anti-Semitism*, Oxford 1983, 188–9.

4. For a recent discussion of Marcion's reading of the Hebrew Scripture and its implications for a Christian doctrine of Judaism, see David P. Efroymson, "The Patristic Connection," in *AntiSemitism and the Foundations of Christianity*, ed. Alan T. Davies, New York 1979, 100–8.

5. The traditional Catholic response to this challenge, defending the Old Testament, appears in five Advent sermons given by Cardinal Faulhaber and published in translation as *Judaism, Christianity, and Germany*, London 1934. Cardinal Faulhaber argues that "Antagonism to the Jews of today must not be extended to the books of pre-Christian Judaism" (14).

6. This can be seen, for example, in the development of a negative attitude toward the Septuagint after the rise of Christianity. "The day on which the Greek translation was made was as painful for Israel as the day of the Golden Calf" (*Sofrim* 1:5); "God foresaw that in days to come the nations of the world would translate the Torah and read it in Greek and say 'We are Israel;'" therefore God refused to allow the Mishnah to be revealed to Moses in a written form (*Tanhuma* Buber, *Va-Yera* 6; see Joseph Heinemann, *Literature of the Synagogue*, New York 1975, 155.

7. The correlation of Marcionism, or more broadly "Gnosticism," with

anti-Jewish tendencies is by no means a simple matter. There is no evidence of explicitly anti-Jewish doctrine in what is known of Marcion's writings. Tertullian's *Adversus Marcionem* reveals a complex dialectic. In defending the rationality and justice of the Mosaic commandments against Marcion's view that they were intended by the Creator to enslave the human race (Book 2), he uses arguments that could have been (and indeed were) used by Jews against Christian detractors of the law. Yet in arguing that the prophecies of the Old Testament were fulfilled by Jesus against Marcion's view that the Old Testament prophesied a different redeemer who has not yet come (Book 3), Tertullian uses arguments that could have been (and indeed were) used against the Jews. Marcion agreed with the Jews that the messiah prophesied in the Old Testament had not yet come; Marcion used this to reject the Old Testament, Jews to reject the New Dispensation. Cf. the review of this issue by Efroymson, loc. cit., and Gager, 162–7.

8. See Robert L. Wilken, "Early Christian Chiliasm, Jewish Messianism, and the Idea of the Holy Land," in *Christians Among Jews and Gentiles*, ed. George Nickelsburg with George MacRae, Philadelphia 1986, 298–307. Wilken is currently working on the shift of Christian attitudes toward the "Holy Land" in the fourth century.

9. For the "spiritualization" of the land in the Christian sources of the church fathers, see Wilken's article noted above. For a penetrating and nuanced analysis of the New Testament which reveals that positive attitudes toward holy space remained alongside the tendencies to de-emphasize and abandon this category, see W. D. Davies, *The Gospel and the Land*, Berkeley and Los Angeles 1974.

10. See the discussion of demographics by S. W. Baron, *A Social and Religious History of the Jews* = *SRHJ* 1, Philadelphia 1952, 170–1.

11. A recent popular discussion of the effects of the defeat is in Yehoshafat Harkabi, *The Bar Kokhba Syndrome*, Chappaqua, NY 1983, 45–53.

12. See Gerhart Ladner, "Aspects of Patristic Anti-Judaism," in *Images and Ideas in the Middle Ages*, 2 vols, Rome 1983, 868.

13. "The Homily on the Passion," ed. C. Bonner, *Studies and Documents* 12, 1940, 179; Stuart Hall (ed.), *Melito of Sardes: On Pascha and Fragments*, Oxford 1979, 51–5. On this work, see Eric Werner, "Melito of Sardes, The First Poet of Deicide," *HUCA*, 37, 1966, 191–210.

14. For a popular assessment of the excavations at Sardis, see Gager, *The Origins of Anti-Semitism*, 99–101.

15. St John Chrysostom, Discourse 1.3.3, 1.4.2, in Wayne Meeks and Robert Wilken, *Jews and Christians in Antioch in the First Four Centuries of the Common Era*, Missoula 1978, 90, 92; *Discourses Against Judaizing Christians*, trans. Paul Harkins, Washington DC 1979, 11, 15. See the fine discussion by Robert Wilken, *John Chrysostom and the Jews: Rhetoric and Reality in the Late Fourth Century*, Berkeley 1983. The association of synagogue, Jews, and the demonic, rooted in the New Testament (John 8:44, Revelation 2:9, 3:9), would become a topos of medieval and early modern anti-Judaism.

16. Amnon Linder, *The Jews in Roman Imperial Legislation*, Detroit 1987, 124–32 (including a justification for the dating of this decree in 329 rather than the traditional 315).

Notes

17. On the treatment of pagans through the fourth century, see Robin Lane Fox, *Pagans and Christians*, London and New York 1987, 609–81; for a broader picture, see Johannes Geffcken, *The Last Days of Greco-Roman Paganism*, Amsterdam, New York and Oxford 1978 (quotation is from p. 120).

18. Timothy Barnes, *Constantine and Eusebius*, Cambridge, MA 1981, 224; W. H. C. Frend, *The Rise of Christianity*, London and Philadelphia 1984, 620, 639–40.

19. The position of Ambrose is stated in the context of an actual incident: he denounces the Emperor Theodosius for ordering that a synagogue in Asia Minor destroyed in an anti-Jewish riot be rebuilt by the local bishop. In his letter he states that it would indeed be a glorious act to burn down the synagogue of Milan, "that there might be no place where Christ is denied." This is not quite a theoretical repudiation of toleration, and extraneous issues such as the relationship between imperial and episcopal power are involved, but Ambrose seems to be placing the Jews in the same category as heretics. See James Parkes, *The Conflict of the Church and the Synagogue*, London, Cleveland, New York and Philadelphia 1961, 166–68, and Ladner, "Aspects of Patristic Anti-Judaism," 867–70.

20. Relevant passages are published in J. Stevenson (ed.), *Creeds, Councils and Controversies*, London 1966, 211–12. The scriptural basis for this position is Luke 14:23: "Compel them to come in," and the conversion of Paul, an act of coercion imposed on Paul against his will. Augustine states that he had originally been opposed to the use of force against heretics in the belief that it would never make sincere Christians, but he was persuaded to the contrary by effective suppression of the Donatists. Cf. the discussion in Frend, 670–3.

21. Augustine's comments on the Jews are scattered throughout his writings, but the most important passages are in his *Reply to Faustus the Manichean*, Book 12, paragraphs 9–13 (the passage is included in Frank Talmage, *Disputation and Dialogue*, New York 1975, 28–32); *The City of God*, Book 4, chapter 34 and Book 18, chapter 46; *Exposition on the Psalms* on Ps. 59:18–19. For a comprehensive discussion, see Bernhard Blumenkranz, *Die Judenpredigt Augustins*, Basle 1946.

22. On this particular motif in Augustine and other Christian writers, see Ruth Mellinkoff, *The Mark of Cain*, Berkeley 1981.

23. A good example of Augustine's influence is the beginning of Innocent III's letter to the Count of Nevers, dated 17 January 1208: "The Lord made Cain a wanderer and a fugitive over the earth, but set a mark upon him, making his head to shake, lest any finding him should slay him. Thus the Jews, against whom the blood of Jesus Christ calls out, although they ought not be killed, lest the Christian people forget the Divine Law, yet as wanderers ought they to remain upon the earth, until their countenance be filled with shame and they seek the name of Jesus Christ, the Lord." Solomon Grayzel, *The Church and the Jews in the XIIIth Century*, New York, 1966, 127. Cf. also the discussion of St Bernard, below.

24. Quoted in Alexander Altmann, *Moses Mendelssohn*, University of Alabama 1973, 212.

25. Jacob Neusner, *Judaism and Christianity in the Age of Constantine*, Chicago 1987.

26. Cf. Neusner, 27.

27. Abraham ben David in *Zikhron Divrei Romi*; cf. Gerson Cohen, *The Book of Tradition by Abraham ibn Daud*, Philadelphia 1967, xxxiii.

28. See the review by Jacob Lauterbach, "Jesus in the Talmud," *Rabbinic Essays*, Cincinnati 1951, 477–570.

29. Jacob Katz, *Exclusiveness and Tolerance*, Oxford 1961, 24–47.

2. The High Middle Ages

1. The text, from the year 591, is readily accessible in Jacob Marcus, *The Jew in the Medieval World*, New York 1965, 111–12. On Gregory's policy toward the Jews, cf. James Parkes, *The Conflict of Church and Synagogue*, 210–21; Edward A. Synan, *The Popes and the Jews in the Middle Ages*, New York 1965, 35–50; S. W. Baron, *SRHJ* 3, Philadelphia, 1957, 27–32. See also G. R. Evans, *The Thought of Gregory the Great*, Cambridge 1986, 135–8.

2. On the meaning of *superstitio* in contemporary Latin usage, see Synan, *The Popes and the Jews in the Middle Ages*, 37, and Linder, *The Jews in Roman Imperial Legislation*, 56–7, 105–6, n. 11.

3. This underlying principle that even involuntary converts, once baptized, could not return to their former creed, was explicitly stated in 633 by the Fourth Toledan Council under the leadership of Isidore of Seville; see Baron, *SRHJ*, 3:39. The text is translated in Robert Chazen, *Church, State, and Jew in the Middle Ages*, New York 1980, 20–1. Roman imperial legislation from the early fifth century permitted Jews who converted out of insincere motives to return to Judaism: see Linder, 275–6.

4. Thomas Aquinas, *Summa Theologica*, II–II Q. 11, Art. 3. On the other hand, Aquinas defended the traditional prohibition of forced baptism, specifically pertaining to Jewish children (II–II Q. 10, Art. 12), appealing to the age-old custom of the church, the probability that such children will be persuaded by their parents to return to Judaism, and the principle of "natural justice."

5. See Solomon Katz, *The Jews in the Visigothic and Frankish Kingdoms of Spain and Gaul*, 1937; reprint: New York 1970; Parkes, *Conflict*, 345–70; Baron, *SRHJ*, 3:36–46; Bernard S. Bachrach, *Early Medieval Jewish Policy in Western Europe*, Minneapolis 1977, 3–26.

6. Bachrach, 133–6.

7. This paragraph represents the conclusions of Bernhard Blumenkranz, *Juifs et chrétiens dans le monde occidental, 430–1096*, Paris 1960. The more radical thesis of Arthur Zuckerman, *A Jewish Princedom in Feudal France: 768–900*, New York 1972, arguing that Jews under Carolingian kings were assigned a territory of their own and permitted to live as an autonomous principality under their own political leader, has not been generally accepted by other scholars.

8. See Dana Carleton Munro, "The Speech of Pope Urban II at Clermont, 1095," *The American Historical Review*, 11, 1906, 231–42.

9. This argument is attributed to the Christians in all three Hebrew chronicles of the First Crusade. For a similar statement in a Christian text, see *Self and Society in Medieval France: The Memoirs of Abbot Guibert of Nogent*, ed. John Benton, New York 1970, 134–5. The Hebrew chronicles are available

Notes

in English translation, together with annotation and analysis, in Shlomo Eidelberg, *The Jews and the Crusaders*, Madison 1977, and Robert Chazan, *European Jewry and the First Crusade*, Berkeley, CA 1987. Cf. also Baron, *SRHJ* 4, Philadelphia 1957, 89–116, and Ivan Marcus, "From Politics to Martyrdom," *Prooftexts* 2, 1982, 40–52.

10. This has been suggested by Sylvia Shein, "The Crusades as a Messianic Movement" (Hebrew), in *Meshihiyut ve-Eschatologiyah*, ed. Zvi Baras, Jerusalem 1983, 177–89. Cf. Norman Cohn, *The Pursuit of the Millennium*, New York 1970, 67–70.

11. Chazan, *Church, State and Jews in the Middle Ages*, 60–3; Baron, *SRHJ*, 4:68, 102, and 290 n. 15; Steven Runciman, *A History of the Crusades*, 3 vols., London and New York 1964, 1:136.

12. See Baron's discussion of the number killed (*SRHJ*, 4:105), concluding that "there is no way of ascertaining the real number of victims." 5000 therefore represents an order of magnitude, not a precise calculation. Compare, however, the statement in a pamphlet published by the Department on Interreligious Affairs of the Union of American Hebrew Congregations in the spring of 1986: "Approximately 1,000,000 Jews were killed by marauding Crusaders who were too cowardly to risk the seas and to face a well-armed enemy in the Holy Land, and so they chose to pillage and rape in the ghettos of Europe instead." This is an example of history transformed into mythos.

13. This has become a controversial point in recent Jewish historiography. For the argument against conceptualizing 1096 as a watershed in medieval Jewish history, see Chazan, *European Jewry and the First Crusade*, 199–211.

14. Baron, *SRHJ*, 4:106; James Parkes, *The Jew in the Mediaeval Community*, London 1938, 79–81. The status within the Jewish community of those Jews who had converted under duress became a matter for authorities in Jewish law to work out. On the general problem, see Jacob Katz, *Exclusiveness and Tolerance*, 67–76.

15. Bernard's "Letter to the People of England," in Chazan, *Church, State, and Jew in the Middle Ages*, 103. This passage also refers to Christian moneylenders who *peius judaizare*, "Judaize worse", than the Jews. This is apparently the first usage of the verb in the negative sense implying greed for financial gain at the expense of others. See Baron, 4:121 and 301 n. 42. For a comprehensive treatment, see David Berger, "The Attitude of St. Bernard of Clairvaux Toward the Jews," *PAAJR* 40, 1972, 89–108.

16. A prime example is the thought of German Pietism (*Hasidut Ashkenaz*). See Katz, 93–105. Kabbalah, the main medieval Jewish mystical tradition, developed this negative evaluation of the Gentile even further, in a manner that might properly be characterized as demonization, but it arose in a different geographical milieu, without any apparent influence by the experience of the Crusades.

17. Cf. Edward Flannery, *The Anguish of the Jews*, New York 1965, xi.

18. A. Jessopp and M. R. James, *The Life and Miracles of St William of Norwich by Thomas of Monmouth*, Cambridge 1896; quotations in the following paragraph of the text are taken from 93–4 and 42. Excerpts from this work are included in Marcus, *The Jew in the Medieval World*, 115–26, and Chazan,

Church, State, and Jew, 141–5, 152–7. An important study of this work has been undertaken by Gavin Langmuir, "Thomas of Monmouth: Detector of Ritual Murder," *Speculum* 59, 1984, 820–46; cf. also his "The Knight's Tale of Young Hugh of Lincoln," *Speculum* 47, 1972, 459–82. For a still valuable overview of the ritual murder accusation and blood libel see Hermann Strack, *The Jew and Human Sacrifice*, New York 1909, and Joshua Trachtenberg, *The Devil and the Jews*, 1943; reprint: Philadelphia 1983, 124–55. An impressive new treatment which focuses on a somewhat later period is R. Po-Chia Hsia, *The Myth of Ritual Murder: Jews and Magic in Reformation Germany*, New Haven 1988; see the other literature mentioned there on 2 n. 3.

19. See Origen, *Contra Celsum*, ed. Henry Chadwick, Cambridge 1953, 343 and note 1 for other ancient sources. This material was known by Jews at least from the late fifteenth century, and used in responding to the libel. See David Ruderman, *The World of a Renaissance Jew*, Cincinnati 1981, 53, on Elijah Delmedigo, referring to Origen's *Contra Celsum*, as well as Tertullian and Thomas Aquinas (the passage is quoted on 195 n. 87). It is also intriguing to note that medieval Persian Christians were accused by Mandeans of killing Jewish children and using their blood in bread. See Baron, *SRHJ*, 3:160.

20. Innocent IV, in Solomon Grayzel, *The Church and the Jews in the XIIIth Century*, 271.

21. The most recent treatment is by Hsia, *The Myth of Ritual Murder*, 43–50. Here the reason given in a contemporary poem is simply that the Jews "must have Christian blood in this Easter time." Hsia's book documents the confusion among fifteenth- and sixteenth-century Germans over the reason for the alleged need of Christian blood, including a suggestion made by the eminent scholar Johannes Eck that God's curse caused Jewish males to suffer menstruation, which could be cured only by Christian blood (130). This insight is (erroneously) attributed to St Augustine.

22. See my *Decoding the Rabbis*, Cambridge 1980, 3–5, and the literature cited there.

23. Relevant documents are conveniently accessible in Chazan, *Church, State and Jew*, 221–38. For a general review of the campaign and its aftermath, see, most recently, Jeremy Cohen, *The Friars and the Jews: The Evolution of Medieval Anti-Judaism*, Ithaca and London 1982, 60–85.

24. Allan and Helen Cutler, *The Jew As Ally of the Muslim*, Notre Dame 1986. The book makes an important case for studying papal Jewish policy in a broader context, and it is valuable for its rich bibliographical discussions, but the thesis is deeply flawed. One could make a comparable argument that Nazi antisemitism was really only an "internal form" of hatred and fear of the Russians and find many links between Jews and Bolsheviks in Nazi literature to sustain it. But both medieval anti-Jewish sentiment and modern antisemitism are documented by many texts that have no relationship to an external threat. The association with an external enemy is a symptom of the prejudice, not its primary cause.

25. Jeremy Cohen, *The Friars and the Jews* (see n. 23 above). This argument minimizes twelfth-century developments, popular forms of anti-Jewish thinking, and social forces in favor of the doctrines of the intellectual leaders of Christianity.

Notes

26. Lester K. Little, *Religious Poverty and the Profit Economy in Medieval Europe*, London 1978. A recent work which makes a similar argument is Jacques Le Goff, *Your Money or Your Life: Economy and Religion in the Middle Ages*, New York 1988. Documenting the tension between the needs of the new monetary economy and the traditional Christian values through confessors' manuals and preachers' *exempla*, Le Goff notes that the Jew was branded as the paradigmatic usurer even though the number of Christian usurers was dramatically increasing (35–9).

27. R. I. Moore, *The Formation of a Persecuting Society: Power and Deviance in Western Europe, 950–1250*, Oxford 1987. John Boswell, *Christianity, Social Tolerance and Homosexuality*, Chicago 1980, 269–302, treats the greater intolerance toward Jews in the context of similar shifts in attitudes toward (and legislation regarding) gay people. The comparative dimension is also emphasized, for a somewhat later period, by H. R. Trevor-Roper, *The European Witch-Craze of the Sixteenth and Seventeenth Centuries*, London and New York 1969, 109–112, 150, 186. The thesis is concisely summarized on 110: "In its periods of introversion and social intolerance Christian society, like any society, looks for scapegoats. Either the Jew or the witch will do, but society will settle for the nearest." R. I. Moore's argument about the exploitation of the persecuting impulse by centralized bureaucracies can be buttressed by the evidence that anti-Jewish initiatives were the first attempts by the Capetian monarchs to legislate for their entire realms. See the work of Gavin Langmuir, incorporated by Robert Chazan into his *Medieval Jewry in Northern France*, Baltimore 1973, 100–41.

28. Most serious historians today have followed S. W. Baron in repudiating what he called the "lachrymose conception of Jewish history" (*History and Jewish Historians*, Philadelphia 1964, 84 and 96, and frequently elsewhere in his work). Cf. Peter Riesenberg, "Jews in the Structure of Western Institutions," *Judaism* 28, 1979, 402–15. The older view is represented by a statement written by Friedrich Heer: "Measured in terms of duration, magnitude and conscious suffering there is nothing in the history of Europe, or even of the world, to compare with the martyrdom of the Jews of medieval Europe" (*The Medieval World*, New York 1963, 312). Though undoubtedly well-intentioned, that this could be written by an esteemed German historian after the Holocaust is indeed extraordinary.

29. The above statements are documented in my "Christians and Jews – Some Positive Images," in *Christians Among Jews and Gentiles*, ed. George Nickelsburg with George MacRae, 236–46.

30. Heiko Oberman, *The Roots of Anti-Semitism in the Age of Renaissance and Reformation*, Philadelphia 1984, 95.

31. Rudiger, in Chazan, *Church, State, and Jew*, 58; George, in Oberman, 96.

3. The Age of the Reformation

1. The classic and still authoritative treatment of the 1391 riots and their aftermath is Yitzhak Baer, *A History of the Jews in Christian Spain*, 2 vols., Philadelphia 1966, 2, 95–169. Whether these riots should be conceptualized primarily as anti-Jewish expressions of mass religious fervor or as social uprisings in which the anti-Jewish element was central has been investigated

by recent historians; see Philippe Wolff, "The 1391 Pogrom in Spain: Social Crisis or Not?" *Past and Present* 50, 1967, 4–18.

2. For an interesting assessment of the role of the *conversos* by a modern Spanish historian, see Americo Castro, *The Spaniards*, Berkeley 1971, 147–60.

3. The definitive treatment of this subject is Albert Sicroff, *Les controverses des statuts de pureté de sang en Espagne du XVe au XVIIe siècle*, Paris 1960. For a brief overview, see Joseph Kaplan, "Jews and Judaism in the Political and Social Thought of Spain in the Sixteenth and Seventeenth Centuries," in *Antisemitism Through the Ages*, ed. Shmuel Almog, New York 1988, 153–60. A possible adumbration of the "racial" definition of the Jew can be found in the controversy over the papal candidacy of Anacletus II in 1130, in which opponents referred disparagingly to the Jewish ancestry of Anacletus. See Aryeh Grabois, "From 'Theological' to 'Racial' Hatred of the Jews in the Twelfth-Century Controversy over the 'Jewish' Pope" [in Hebrew], *Zion* 47, 1982, 1–16.

4. Baer, *A History of the Jews in Christian Spain*, 2:324–423.

5. For a recent review of the relevant bibliography, see Allan and Helen Cutler, *The Jew as Ally of the Muslim*, 481–4. Important overviews of the methodological issues can be found in Francisco Marquez Villaneuva, "The Converso Problem: an Assessment," in *Collected Studies in Honor of Americo Castro's Eightieth Year*, ed. M. P. Hornik, Oxford 1965, 317–33, and Yosef Yerushalmi, *From Spanish Court to Italian Ghetto*, New York and London 1971, 21–31.

6. Matthew Spinka, *John Hus at the Council of Constance*, New York and London 1965, 230; Louis I. Newman, *Jewish Influence on Christian Reform Movements*, New York 1925, 437; Baron, *SRHJ* 13, New York and London 1969, 212, 215–16.

7. Baron, 13:92, 274–75; Selma Stern, *Josel of Rosheim*, Philadelphia 1965, 95; Hsia, *The Myth of Ritual Murder*, 131; Martin Luther, "That Jesus Christ was Born a Jew," in *Luther's Works*, 55 vols., St Louis 1958 – Philadelphia 1967, 45: 197, 199.

8. See Norman Cohn, *Warrant for Genocide*, Chico, CA 1981, 45–6; the original Spanish text is reprinted in Sicroff, *Les controverses*, 116–17.

9. Luther, "That Jesus Christ Was Born a Jew," 200.

10. Luther, *Table Talk*, in *Luther's Works*, 54:436–37 (section 5504).

11. Luther, *On the Jews and their Lies*, in *Luther's Works*, 47:161.

12. Luther, "Against the Sabbatarians," in *Luther's Works*, 47:66.

13. Luther, *Lies*, 269.

14. Quoted in Haim Hillel Ben Sasson, "The Reformation in Contemporary Jewish Eyes," *Proceedings of the Israel Academy of Sciences and Humanities* 4, 1970, 292.

15. Oberman, *The Roots of Anti-Semitism*, p. 118; Baron, *SRHJ*, 13:243, 245; Luther, "Sabbatarians," 65. Cf. Benjamin Nelson, *The Idea of Usury*, Chicago 1969, 36–45, 52, 58. For the contemporary Jewish outlook on these groups, cf. Jerome Friedman, "The Reformation in Alien Eyes," *The Sixteenth Century Journal* 14, 1983, 29.

16. Calvin, "On God and Political Duty," in *On Civil Government*, ed. John McNeill, Indianapolis 1956, 45.

17. Baron, *SRHJ*, 13:283–5.

18. This rhetorical technique of trying to discredit religious positions by branding them as under the influence of the Jews was not unique to the Reformation. It was widely used in antiquity in the context of theological debates (see Baron, *SRHJ*, 3:5–7). It was also used in internal Muslim polemics attacking Shi'ites, Fatimids, and, in modern times, Young Turks. See Baron, *SRHJ*, 3:147; S. D. Goitein, *Jews and Arabs*, New York 1964, 147–8; Bernard Lewis, *The Jews of Islam*, Princeton 1984, 103–4, and *Semites and Anti-Semites*, New York 1986, 138.

19. Martin A. Cohen, *Usque's Consolation for the Tribulations of Israel*, Philadelphia 1964, 193. The subject of Jewish perceptions of the Reformation is treated in the above-cited articles by Ben Sasson and Friedman.

20. See Ben Sasson, 267–8.

21. Cf. Ben Sasson, 269, 278; Baron, 13:219, 249. For the role of millenarian thinking in Luther's outlook on the Jews, see Oberman, 116–22.

22. Luther, *Lies*, 167, 291. This assertion caused an uproar when made by a leading evangelical Christian spokesman a few years ago.

23. Luther, "Sabbatarians," 66, cf. 79, 83–4. For the argument in Chrysostom, see Discourse 4.4.4–4.5.6, 5.1.5, 5.4.1.

24. Luther, "Sabbatarians," 80; *Lies*, 224. Cf. also his sarcastic recommendation, "No one is holding them here now. The country and the roads are open for them to proceed to their land whenever they wish. If they did so, we would be glad to present gifts to them on the occasion; it would be good riddance" (*Lies*, 265).

25. Luther, *Lies*, 167 (first two quotations), 264, 277, 275, 261.

26. Luther, *Lies*, 256, 212. On the image of Jews eating the turds of a sow or nursing from the sow, see Trachtenberg, frontispiece, and Isaiah Shachar, *The Judensau*, London 1974. Quotations from Luther's *Vom Schem Hamphoras*, which has not been translated in *Luther's Works*, appear on 44, 86–7. Luther was not unique in heaping scatalogical ridicule upon the Jews, as can be seen in the German literature of the time: Hsia, *The Myth of Ritual Murder*, 64, 213–14 n. 57.

27. Luther, *Lies*, 268–72.

28. Luther, *Lies*, 267.

29. Quoted in Oberman, 121; Baron, *SRHJ*, 13:228.

30. Explaining the apparently radical shift between Luther's 1523 tract and his 1543 tract on the Jews has challenged many historians; it is obviously of more than mere antiquarian interest. Some have viewed the 1540s writings as a sign of sickness or senility. Others have emphasized different factors: his bitter disappointment over the failure of Jews to convert to his purified Christianity, his need to defend his movement from the Catholic attack of Judaizing, the traditional loyalty of the Jews to the Catholic emperor who impeded the progress of the Lutheran Reformation, and the impact of the book *Der gantz jüdisch Glaub* (The Entire Jewish Faith) by the apostate Antonius Margaritha, a book which furnished Luther with considerable ammunition. See Baron, *SRHJ*, 13:221–26, with accompanying notes. More recently there has been a tendency to deny a sharp reversal by noting anti-Jewish motifs in Luther's earliest work and emphasizing the rhetorical

function of the positive statements in "That Jesus Christ Was Born a Jew."
This case has been made compellingly by Oberman, 104–7.

31. Quoted in Ben Sasson, 287–8.

32. Josel of Rosheim, *Sefer ha-Miqnah*, ed. Hava Fraenkel-Goldschmidt,
Jerusalem 1970, quoted in Ben Sasson, 291; cf. Stern, 223–4.

33. For a review of these events, see Baron, *SRHJ*, 14:2–146, and Kenneth
Stow, *Catholic Thought and Papal Jewry Policy*, New York 1977, 3–59. Stow's thesis
is that intense millenarian speculation in the middle of the sixteenth century
engendered a fundamental reversal of the traditional Christian doctrine of
toleration and an aggressive campaign to foster the mass conversion of the
Jews.

34. Joshua Soncino, *Nahalah li-Yhoshu'ah*, Constantinople 1731, p. 45a, col.
2. For the context of this statement, see my "Martyrs, Merchants and Rabbis:
Jewish Communal Conflict as Reflected in the Responsa on the Boycott of
Ancona," *Jewish Social Studies* 43, 1981, 215–28.

35. Joseph ha-Kohen; see Ben Sasson, 283–5.

36. See Baron, *SRHJ*, 13:292–6.

4. The Church and the Holocaust

1. Significant efforts to assess the implications of the Holocaust on Christian
belief can be seen, for example, in Rosemary Ruether, *Faith and Fratricide*, New
York 1974, esp. 246–61; Franklin Littell, *The Crucifixion of the Jews*, New York
1975; Gregory Baum, *Christian Theology after Auschwitz*, London 1976; Michael
McGarry, *Christology After Auschwitz*, New York 1977; John Pawlikowski, *Christ
in the Light of the Christian–Jewish Dialogue*, Ramsey, N J 1982, esp. 136–47;
A. Roy Eckardt with Alice Eckardt, *Long Night's Journey into Day: Life and Faith
After the Holocaust*, Detroit 1982.

2. Hyam Maccoby's statement may be taken as a paradigm for this
approach: "As a result of the Gospel story, the Jews were made into an outcast,
accursed nation in Christendom and were persecuted in all Christian lands.
The massacre of 6 million Jews in Nazi Europe was only the most recent and
worst of these persecutions" (*New Society*, 6 January 1983). Cf. the assessment of
one of the leading Christian authorities on the history of anti-Jewish doctrine,
James Parkes: "More than six million deliberate murders are the consequence
of the teachings about Jews for which the Christian Church is ultimately
responsible, and of an attitude to Judaism which is not only maintained by all
the Christian churches, but has its ultimate resting place in the teaching of the
New Testament itself" (quoted in Byron Sherwin, *Encountering the Holocaust*,
Chicago 1979, 34–5).

3. Martin Bertram, introduction to *On the Jews and their Lies, Luther's Works*,
47:136. Cf. Baron, *SRHJ*, 13:428 n. 24. For Nazi historians and propagandists,
the positive statements in "That Jesus Christ was Born a Jew" were a source of
embarrassment. Heiko Oberman cites the following statement by Martin
Sasse, published in 1938: "In this hour [1543] we hear the voice of the German
prophet of the sixteenth century, who out of ignorance began his career as a
friend of the Jews, and who, driven by his conscience, his experience and by
reality, became the greatest anti-Semite of his age, and warned his nation
against the Jews." *The Roots of Anti-Semitism*, 128, n. 26.

4. In a seminar on Christian–Jewish relations which I co-taught with Professor Krister Stendahl at Harvard Divinity School, Prof. Stendahl showed a copy of this pamphlet, translated into Swedish, which had been distributed door to door by Nazi sympathizers.

5. *The Jew in the Modern World*, ed. Paul Mendes-Flohr and Jehuda Reinharz, Oxford 1980, 282 and 284 n. 11. Luther, *On the Jews and their Lies*, 275.

6. Luther, *Lies*, 266, 292. The quotation from the Nazi physician at Auschwitz, Fritz Klein, is reported by Dr Ella Lingens-Reiner, *Prisoners of Fear*, London 1948, 1–2. On the psychological makeup of this and other SS physicians, see Robert Jay Lifton, *The Nazi Doctors*, New York 1986.

7. *Der Stuermer*, May 1934. This entire edition has been reproduced in *The Holocaust: Selected Documents in Eighteen Volumes*, ed. John Mendelsohn, New York 1982, 4:92–111. A translation of the text with the original picture and format was published in *Christian Vanguard*, February 1976, 3. A second special edition of *Der Stuermer* entirely devoted to the ritual murder libel was published in May 1939.

8. Nechama Tec, *When Light Pierced the Darkness*, Oxford 1988, 41.

9. *Hitler's Table Talk*, cited by Ruether, *Faith and Fratricide*, 224.

10. Roger Manvell, *SS and Gestapo*, New York 1969, 109, quoted by Irving Greenberg in *Auschwitz; Beginning of a New Era?*, ed. Eva Fleischner, New York 1977, 46. Greenberg comments: "Whenever I reread this passage, I swear that the name of God must be hidden away in absolute silence and secrecy for so long that all the murderers and bystanders will have forgotten it. Only then can it be brought out and used again." *Mein Kampf*, New York 1940, 84; cf. 640.

11. Greenberg, in *Auschwitz: Beginning of a New Era?*, 441. The statement attributed to Archbishop Kametko of Nietra (11–12) is Rabbi Dov Weissmandl's report, written considerably after the war (*Min ha-Meiṣar*, Jerusalem 1960, 24), of a conversation which had been reported to him by the Nietra Rebbe. Weissmandl's unreliability in such matters is conceded by Greenberg on 441–2. The importance of precise distinctions is obvious. Greenberg's formulation that "the Jews deserve their fate" does reflect the traditional doctrine – so long as that fate is understood to be consignment to harsh living conditions. But when the statement is used in the context of the Final Solution, it implies that Christian leaders justified the death camps as a proper punishment, and this is not clearly documented. The distinction is not a mere quibble; it lies at the essence of the questions about the relationship between the Holocaust and Christian doctrine. For another example of a Jewish writer making the leap to an extreme claim without clear justification, see Richard Rubenstein, *After Auschwitz*, Indianapolis, New York and Kansas City 1966, 55–6. For Christian writers, see the Eckardts, *Long Night's Journey into Day*, 61 and 157–8 n. 38.

12. A concise statement of the case for discontinuity is made by Yosef Yerushalmi in his response to Rosemary Ruether, *Auschwitz: Beginning of a New Era?*, 97–107.

13. Merely to list parallels between medieval and Nazi anti-Jewish measures, as Raul Hilberg does in the first chapter of his magisterial work *The Destruction of the European Jews*, is misleading in its emphasis upon similarities at the expense of what was radically new. A case can be made that in the

1930s, the Nazis would have been satisfied with a return to the medieval status. But after the war began, the use of "medieval" institutions such as the ghetto became a ploy to deceive the Jews and the outside world. The differences were recognized by Professor Peter-Heinz Seraphim, a Nazi "expert" on Jewish affairs, who wrote in March 1941: "The ghetto of the Middle Ages was largely a Jewish privilege rather than a forced measure . . . It was a residential community; in addition to which it by no means excluded business contacts between Jews and non-Jews . . . The ghetto of today must be different from the medieval ghetto; it must be a compulsory ghetto . . . without contact or possibility of contact with non-Jews." Quoted by Philip Friedman, *Roads to Extinction: Essays on the Holocaust*, New York and Philadelphia 1980, 64.

14. Dietrich Bonhoeffer, *No Rusty Swords*, ed. Edwin H. Robertson, London and New York 1965, 223, 226; Niemoeller, *Here Stand I*, trans. Jane Lymburn, Chicago and New York 1937, 195.

15. Dietrich Bonhoeffer, *Ethics*, ed. E. Bethge, London and New York 1963, 26–7; cf. *No Rusty Swords*, 226–7. Cf. Rosemary Ruether, *Faith and Fratricide*, 224.

16. Niemoeller, *Here Stand I*, 195.

17. I first encountered a citation of this sermon in Tec, *When Light Pierced the Darkness*, 10, which refers to Helen Fein, *Accounting for Genocide*, New York 1979, 115, which refers to Johan M. Snoek, *The Grey Book*, Assen 1969, 181–2, which (on 182–3) refers to Benjamin Arditi, *Les juifs de Bulgarie sous le régime Nazi, 1940–44* [in Hebrew], Tel Aviv, 1962, 201–2. Unfortunately, there is no reference to such a sermon or argument on these pages of Arditi. The earlier versions make it clear that the passage, if authentic, must be based on a report of the sermon, not a text written by the preacher.

18. Michael Marrus and Robert Paxton, *Vichy France and the Jews*, New York 1981, 271; cf. Philip Friedman, *Their Brothers' Keepers*, New York 1957, 50.

19. Marrus and Paxton, 272; cf. Friedman, 50.

20. Philip Friedman, *Roads to Extinction*, 431.

21. Philip Hallie, *Lest Innocent Blood be Shed*, New York, 1980.

22. *Notes from the Warsaw Ghetto: The Journal of Emmanuel Ringelblum*, ed. and trans. Jacob Sloan, New York 1974, 117, cf. 186. (Friedman, *Roads to Extinction*, 431, notes a 1944 Gestapo report complaining, "From various places we hear that priests have recently begun to praise Jewry very highly in their sermons.")

23. Tec, *When Light Pierced the Darkness*, 103–4.

24. From *Pinkas Novy-Dvor*, trans. in Jack Kugelmass and Jonathan Boyarin, *From a Ruined Garden*, New York 1983, 178.

25. Guenter Lewy, *The Catholic Church and Nazi Germany*, New York and Toronto 1964, 78. Lewy discusses the concordat at great length.

26. On the "euthanasia" program and the resistance to it by religious figures, see, most recently, Lifton, *The Nazi Doctors*, 45–95. This has been frequently cited as an example of the Nazi regime's susceptibility to pressure emanating from public opinion mobilized by religious leaders.

27. John Morley, *Vatican Diplomacy and the Jews During the Holocaust*, New York 1980, 112, 114.

Notes

28. Morley, 92–3. For other expressions of anti-Zionist sentiment in the context of the possible rescue of Jews, see ibid., 94, 206.

29. On the October 1943 roundup of Rome's Jews, see Susan Zuccotti, *The Italians and the Holocaust*, New York 1987, 101–38. The private protest by the Cardinal Secretary of State became known only with the Vatican's release of documents from its archives covering the year 1943. The German ambassador to the Vatican, Baron Ernst von Weizsäcker, reported to his Foreign Ministry that "although under pressure from all sides, the Pope has not allowed himself to be drawn into any demonstrative censure of the deportation of the Jews of Rome," and has "done all he could in this delicate matter not to strain relations with the German Government and German circles in Rome." See Lewy, 302; Zuccotti, 130.

30. There is a large literature: in addition to Lewy and Morley, see Saul Friedlander, *Pius XII and the Third Reich*, New York 1966; Pinchas Lapide, *Three Popes and the Jews*, New York 1967; Carlo Falconi, *The Silence of Pius XII*, Boston 1970.

31. Morley, 119.

32. Letter quoted by Father A. Martini, SJ, in Delores and Earl Schmidt, *The Deputy Reader*, Glenview, IL 1965, 175.

33. Cf. David Engel, "The Western Allies and the Holocaust," in *Polin* 1, 1986, 312.

34. Cf. the statement of Yosef Yerushalmi: "My bill of particulars concerning Pius XII . . . is based on the fact that he *broke*, in essence, with the tradition of the medieval popes. It is precisely because the medieval papacy managed to speak out for the Jews *in extremis* that the silence of the Vatican during World War II is all the more deafening." See *Auschwitz: Beginning of a New Era?*, 104.

35. See Lewy, 295–6; *The Deputy Reader*, 158, 164, 175.

36. *The Deputy Reader*, 187.

37. Edoardo Senatro, quoting the Pope, cited in Lewy, 304.

5. Burdens from the Past, Opportunities for the Future

1. *Nostra aetate*, in Helga Croner, *Stepping Stones to Further Jewish–Christian Relations*, London and New York 1977, 2. An earlier draft read "rejected or accursed by God or guilty of deicide;" the last four words were rejected, possibly as a result of political pressures by Arab governments and others; see A. Roy Eckardt, *Your People My People*, New York 1974, 49–51. The Vatican gives a different explanation for this decision: see Walter M. Abbott (ed.), *The Documents of Vatican II*, New York 1966, 666 n. 23. On Jewish reactions to this section of *Nostra aetate*, see Marc Tannenbaum, in *Twenty Years of Jewish – Catholic Relations*, ed. Eugene Fisher et al., New York 1986, 51–3.

2. Croner, *Stepping Stones*, 78. The phrase "stood on the side of the persecutors" may signal a reluctance to concede that all too often Christians *were* the persecutors. The World Council of Churches, like the Catholic church, had to overcome considerable opposition to such statements of friendship toward the Jews. See the report of W. A. Visser't Hooft on the 1954 General Assembly, in Littell, *The Crucifixion of the Jews*, 63–4.

3. "Ecumenical Considerations on Jewish–Christian Dialogue," Geneva: World Council of Churches 1983, sec. 3.2, p. 9. The phrase "teachings of contempt" in this and many similar statements shows the enormous influence of Jules Isaac's *The Teaching of Contempt: Christian Roots of Anti-Semitism*, New York 1964.

4. Croner, *Stepping Stones*, 89–90. Cf. the statement by the noted Lutheran scholar Jaroslav Pelikan in his 1971 presidential address to the International Congress for Luther Research: "The time has come for those who study Luther and admire him to acknowledge, more unequivocally and less pugnaciously than they have, that on this issue Luther's thought and language are simply beyond defense. But any such acknowledgement must be based, theologically, on a much more fundamental conviction, namely, that Judaism is not, as Luther and the centuries before him maintained, a "shadow" destined to disappear with the coming of Christianity even though it stubbornly held on to its existence, but a permanent part of the wondrous dispensation of God in human history." Quoted in Littell, *The Crucifixion of the Jews*, 105–6.

5. "A Theological Understanding of the Relationship between Christians and Jews," adopted "for study and reflection" by the 199th General Assembly (1987) of the Presbyterian Church (USA), 8–9. "The Relationship Between the United Church of Christ and the Jewish Community;" this was passed as a resolution in the 1987 "Sixteenth General Synod" of the UCC, and it therefore has a more official status than the Presbyterian document.

6. *New York Times*, 20 August 1987, 9.

7. Croner, *Stepping Stones*, 2.

8. *The Deputy Reader*, 147.

9. Irving Greenberg, in *Auschwitz: Beginning of a New Era?*, 23. Note the striking use of this principle by the Eckardts, *Long Night's Journey into Day*, 138.

10. *The Diaries of Theodor Herzl*, ed. and trans. Marvin Lowenthal, New York 1956, 428–9. I have not been able to determine whether there is confirmation in Vatican documents for this statement, nor have I been able to find evidence that the Vatican opposition to Zionism was ever officially based on the Augustinian doctrine. Note, however, the reaction of Pope Benedict XV to the Balfour Declaration. Appealing to the sacrifice made by the Crusaders, he concluded, "Surely it would be a terrible grief for Us and for all the Christian faithful if infidels were placed in a privileged and prominent position; much more if those most holy sanctuaries of the Christian religion were given to the charge of non-Christians" (cited by Esther Feldblum, *The American Catholic Press and the Jewish State, 1917–1959*, New York 1977, 78.

11. Eugene Fisher has argued (*Commonweal*, 11 January 1985) that the Pope has expressed Vatican recognition of Israel in the following statement from the apostolic letter *Redemptionis Anno* of Good Friday 1984: "For the Jewish people who live in the state of Israel, and who preserve in that land such precious testimonies to their history and their faith, we must ask for the desired security and the due tranquillity that is the prerogative of every

nation." He maintains that the outstanding issue is only that of the level of diplomatic relations, which, he concedes, is of major symbolic importance to the Jewish community.

12. On American Evangelical support for Zionism and Israel from the nineteenth century through the Six Day War, see Yona Malachy, *American Fundamentalism and Israel*, Jerusalem 1978. Another important study of the theological basis for contemporary support is David Rausch, *Zionism Within Early American Fundamentalism 1878–1918*, Lewiston, NY 1980.

13. Henry Siegman, "A Decade of Catholic – Jewish Relations' — A Reassessment," *Journal of Ecumenical Studies* 15, 1978, 252.

14. For strong statements by Christian writers of the distinction between criticism from within and from outside, see Littell, *The Crucifixion of the Jews*, 3, and Eckhardts, *Long Night's Journey into Day*, 106, 120–2. The Eckardts argue that Jews have the right to set special standards for themselves, but that "Christians have no right to inflict spiritual and moral requirements upon the Jewish people that may perpetuate or compound Jewish suffering . . . As long as the Christian community tries to make Israel something special, to trumpet forth that Israel has obligations greater than or different from those of other human beings, the burden of the Christian past will not be lifted" (106).

15. Some recent treatments of this theme (and here I deal with the Hebrew scriptures alone, not the New Testament, which is primarily an internal Christian issue) include Lawrence Boadt, "The Role of Scripture in Catholic–Jewish Relations," in *Twenty Years of Catholic–Jewish Relations*, 89–108; Bruce Waitke, "An Evangelical Christian View of the Hebrew Scriptures," in *Evangelicals and Jews in an Age of Pluralism*, ed. Marc Tanenbaum et al., Grand Rapids 1984, 105–39.

16. David Rausch reports observing an Evangelical seminary graduate writing on the board of a Sunday School class in two columns, JUDAISM/LAW/DEATH/PHARISEES/OLD TESTAMENT and CHRISTIANITY / GRACE / LIFE / SAINTS / NEW TESTAMENT: "What and How Evangelicals Teach About Judaism," in *A Time to Speak: The Evangelical–Jewish Encounter*, ed. James Rudin and Marvin Wilson, Grand Rapids 1987, 81. For more subtle traces of this attitude, see Eugene Fisher, "Research on Christian Teaching Concerning Jews and Judaism," *Journal of Ecumenical Studies* 21, 1984, 421–36, sec. 1.A., "A Latent Marcionite Approach to the Hebrew Scriptures."

17. Vernon C. Grounds, in *Evangelicals and Jews in an Age of Pluralism*, ed. Marc Tanenbaum, 207. The passage continues: "Harsh and grating expressions as to [Judaism's] salvific discontinuity are called for – abrogation, displacement, and negation. And those expressions are set down here, I assure you, with some realization of how harsh and grating they must indeed sound to Jewish ears."

18. The phrase refers to the doctrine that Judaism has been superseded by Christianity, and the Jewish people by the "New Israel," the Christian church. I was once invited to speak at the Evangelical Gordon-Conwell Theological Seminary in South Hamilton, Massachusetts. After my presentation, a member of the faculty contended that in the Evangelical view,

Judaism was like the first stage of a rocket, absolutely necessary to get the rocket off the ground, but reaching a point where it serves no further purpose. I refrained from reminding him that most rockets have three stages, and from asking about the implications of his analogy for the relationship between Christianity and Islam.

19. For the texts from which these quotations are taken, see note 5 above. Repudiation of supersessionist theology is often made with reference to its historical consequences. The Presbyterian document explains that "The long and dolorous history of Christian imperialism, in which the church often justified anti-Jewish acts and attitudes in the name of Jesus, finds its theological base in this teaching" (6). Franklin Littell speaks of the "superseding or displacement myth" as the "cornerstone of Christian Antisemitism," which logically leads to genocide (*The Crucifixion of the Jews*, 2, 30).

20. For example, the Presbyterian document of 1987, after repudiating supersessionism, goes on to affirm that "faithfulness to [our] covenant requires us to call *all* women and men to faith in Jesus Christ" (6, emphasis in the original), and that "Christians are commissioned to witness to the whole world about the good news of Christ's atoning work for both Jew and Gentile." The document seems to reveal a tension that it does not claim fully to resolve. Other Christian thinkers would categorically reject any kind of "mission to the Jews": see Littell, *The Crucifixion of the Jews*, 88; Eckardts, *Long Night's Journey into Day*, 118–19; Paul Van Buren, *Discerning the Way*, New York 1980, 180ff.

21. It is revealing to compare what the "Messianic Jews" communicate to Evangelical Christians with their appeal intended for Jews. A good example is "A Messianic Jew Pleads His Case," by Daniel Juster with Daniel Pawley, *Christianity Today*, 24 April 1981, 22–4. The "case" which the author pleads is the right of Messianic Jews to be considered as full-fledged Christians despite their Judaizing. He asserts that "our basic confession is in conformity with mainstream evangelical Protestant denominations," and affirms "the basic evangelical concepts of the authority of Scripture, salvation by grace through faith, the triune nature of God, the resurrection of Jesus, the Second Coming, and so on." Why then do they retain Jewish "cultural practices"? "It is first in relating culturally to our own people that we might win them to Jesus. Paul's words ring in our ears with authenticity: 'To the Jews I became as a Jew, in order to win the Jews.'"

22. For Jewish reflections on this issue, see the statements by Blu Greenberg and Sanford Seltzer on "Mission, Witness and Proselytization" in *Evangelicals and Jews in an Age of Pluralism*, 226–54.

23. Cf. the Hasidic tale in Martin Buber's *Tales of the Hasidim*, 2 vols. New York 1951, 2:86, in which Moshe Leib of Sasov learns the meaning of love by overhearing two Gentile peasants drinking in an inn. Various forms of this tale, usually concluding with "How can you say you love me if you do not know what gives me pain?" have been cited frequently in the literature of dialogue; see, e.g., the 1975 Report of a Lutheran World Federation Consultation in Croner, *Stepping Stones*, 130.

Index

Eusebius, 11
"Euthanasia" program, 45–6
Evangelicals, 57–8
Expulsions, 25

Fatimids, 73
Faulhaber, Michael von, 65
Ferdinand, King, 28
"Final Solution," 38, 40, 45, 75;
    see also Holocaust
France: expulsion from, 25;
    Holocaust in, 43
Franciscans, 23

Galilee, 4–5
Geneva (Switzerland), 31
Gentile Christians, 2–3
George (Bishop of Speyer), 25
German Pietism (Hasidut Ashkenaz),
    69
Germany: local expulsions in, 25;
    pastoral letter in, 43; bishops in,
    49
Gerstein, Kurt, 46
Ghetto: 16th century, 37;
    "medieval" vs. Nazi-imposed,
    76
Godfrey of Bouillon, 18
Gommy, Jacques, 54
Gratian, Emperor, 9
Gregory I, 14–16
Grueber, Heinrich, 49

Hadrian, Emperor, 5
Hebrew Bible, Hebrew Scripture:
    relation of to Christian scripture,
    3, 65; and synagogue ritual, 7;
    Jews as guardians of, 9–10; and
    reformation, 32–4; and contem-
    porary dialogue, 59–61; transla-
    tion and, 60; see also Old Testa-
    ment
"Hebrew Christians," 62
Hebrew language, 32, 60
Henry IV, Emperor, 17–18
Heresy, Heretics: Marcion's doc-
    trine declared as, 3; imperial
    policy toward, 8–9; Augustine on,

9; Aquinas on, 15; crusade
    against, 18; medieval persecution
    of, 23; Jews as purveyors of, 28
Herzl, Theodor, 56
Himmler, Heinrich, 40
Hitler, Adolf, 40–1, 44, 45
Hochhuth, Rolf: The Deputy, 46, 53
Holocaust, 38–55
Holy Land, 3–4, 16–17, 46, 66;
    see also Israel, land of
Hugh of Lincoln, 21
Hungary: invasion of, 33; papal nun-
    cio in, 46; Pius XII and, 54
Hus, John, 28
Hussites, 26

Innocent III, 41, 67
Inquisition: jurisdiction of, 15;
    Papal, 22, 27; Spanish, 28
Isabella, Queen, 28
Isidore of Seville, 68
Israel, land of, 3–4, 5, 34, 56; see also
    Holy Land; Palestine
Israel, state of, 55–9, 78–9
Italy, 36

Jerome, 65
Jerusalem, 4–5, 17, 34, 56, 58
"Jesus Movement," 1
Jesus of Nazareth, 1–2, 9, 10, 44; in
    Talmud: 12, 22
Jewish Christians, 2–3, 62
"Jews for Jesus," 62, 63
John Paul II, 53, 57
Josel of Rosheim, 35
Joyce, James: Ulysses, 21, 63
"Judaizing": as heresy, 3, 15, 27,
    29–31; as greed, 69
Judea, 4
Julian, Emperor, 8, 12
Justin Martyr, 2, 11
Justinian, Emperor, 8

Kabbalah, 69
Kalonymos ben Meshullam, 18
Kametko (Archbishop of Nietra), 75

Lateran palace, 15

Index